Peggy the Doll

~ A very different haunting ~

© First published in the UK in 2017 All rights reserved.

The contents of this book are subject to international copyright law, and are the intellectual property of the author Jayne Harris.

No part of this publication may be reproduced, interpreted or adapted in any way without prior consent.

ISBN-13: 978 1 5303 2686 0

ISBN-10:1 5303 2686 9

Cover design © Simon Harris

Dedicated to

my Husband and children who continue to be my rock in the stormiest of seas.

"That doll nearly ruined my life, I want to forget it ever existed and I hope God protects you all"

JW

The original owner of Peggy the Doll

Table of Contents

Preface

Acknowledgments

Foreword

Introduction

Chapter 1 ~ The beginning

Chapter 2 ~ My Illness

Chapter 3 ~ The doll goes public

Chapter 4 ~ Hazel Myers

Chapter 5 ~ Religion

Chapter 6 ~ Dogs

Chapter 7 ~ Considerations

Chapter 8 ~ Derby Gaol

Chapter 9~ Peggy meets Zak

Chapter 10 ~ Olivias Stroke

Chapter 11~ "Deadly Possessions" airs

Chapter 12~ Paris...flies again?

Chapter 13 ~ Molly O'Gradys

Chapter 14 ~ A tough decision

Chapter 15 ~ Peggy's new 'Father'

Chapter 16: ~ Witness Testimonies

Conclusion

FAQ's

About the Author

~ Preface ~

I'll start by saying that this book almost didn't get written. I'd been asked on several occasions to do this, to create a document recording this particular case study and while I know that this case is intriguing and worthy of recording, part of me has continually held back. Exactly why, I'm not too sure. But eventually, in late 2015 I decided it was time to get this down on paper, possibly for fear of forgetting some of the details myself in years to come, or if, as I've been told several times - my dabbling in the unexplained will ultimately seal my own fate, then I would like to know that the work we've done, the experiences we've had and the evidence we've gathered in relation to this doll, will not be lost in the mists of time.

At the time of writing this book I had, along with my Husband and Co-founder Simon, amassed around 17 years of experience dealing with cases of suspected paranormal activity, usually involving supposedly haunted objects, or as I often describe it Spirit Attachment. By this, I don't claim that ghosts or spirits can be trapped inside a material object, which is often the misconception, but that if we believe a building has the ability to absorb, retain and replay thoughts, emotions and events from those who went before us, then why not smaller items too. Infact in many cases it makes far more sense that a treasured possession, something that held a particular significance for someone in life, should have absorbed something of that person. It is my belief that in some way this is how the psychic ability of Psychometry is explained. I believe it is not only people that have an energy field, but objects and places too. We are all part of a huge swirling cosmos of energy, data and memories...to some degree.

Some people can pick up on the energy fields of others more readily than most and we call these people Psychic Mediums.

My first book, co-written with Dan Weatherer, detailed some of my more memorable cases and gave a brief insight, a toe dipped into the water if you like, into the work we do as an organisation. It was with bittersweet irony that as that first book was completed and sent away to the publishers, that the doll now referred to as Peggy came into our lives. Fate has a curious way of handling the timing of events.

This doll, like no other object we have worked with, before or since, has the ability to unnerve and intrigue in equal measure. As our studies progress and our experiences grow, we find ourselves left with more questions than answers. Maybe in reading this book you too will be left with questions, and that's not a bad thing. By it's very nature the world of the paranormal is unexplained, and to some degree eternally unexplainable!

For me, it's probably why I love it so much and why I have devoted my life to it, in more ways than one.

Some names in this book have been altered to protect the identities of those involved. All events and statements are genuine and unexaggerated. I will, for the most part, refer to the doll as Peggy, although in reality that name didn't enter the frame until February 2015. Prior to this she was actually known as "the doll" in our home. Whilst writing each chapter, I found myself still open mouthed at some of the things that have actually happened in relation to this doll, largely by members of the public or people with no links to us or reasons for fabrication. In documenting these I hope to not only raise awareness of what is truly a genuine, paranormal phenomena, but also to give those who have been affected by the spirits or energies associated with the doll known as Peggy, a voice. A place their stories will be immortalised and remembered, and who knows, maybe someone somewhere will read this book one day and will get in touch with me and fill in the gaps!

Until then however, I remain intrigued, a little unnerved and forever learning.

Jayne Harris

Co-Founder & Lead Investigator HD Paranormal Ltd

~ Acknowledgments ~

This book, and indeed the case study into Peggy, owes a debt of gratitude to many people. I would like to thank everyone who has taken time out of their busy lives to get in touch with us over the course of the past 18 months, to let us know their feelings towards Peggy and their experiences. Members of the public are what makes this line of work 'real' for us and without connecting with so many of you, all over the world, we would have merely a fraction of the knowledge and data we now have so thank you.

I would like to acknowledge Paul Stevenson, editor of Haunted Magazine. Paul has been a great friend to me over the last few years, and together with Andy Soar has always supported my work, featuring Peggys story but also being there for everything and anything else going on.

To Patti Negri, the most spiritual woman I've ever met, a fountain of knowledge and experience not to mention a wonderfully warm and caring woman into the bargain. It's a pleasure to know you.

To fellow paranormal 'sufferer' and author Anthony Quinata for the endless – sometimes all day- chats about Peggy, the comparisons and possible connections to Harold and this whole crazy phenomenon.

Special thanks to Ian Griffiths and Paul Bosworth for their friendship and fun approach to the paranormal. The only way to make it through in this crazy world is to not take yourself too seriously!

I'd like to also thanks Karen & Eddie Fray and Graham Sansome, Investigators with HD Paranormal for their hard work and commitment. I have a great team!

I cannot thank Hazel Myers enough for devoting a portion of her life to our studies. It's not always been sunshine and roses!

A huge thank you to Zak Bagans for his curiosity and to his team for reaching out, inviting us to Las Vegas, and working with us in our attempts to communicate with the spirit world. Truly an eye opening experience!

Finally, to my Husband and co-founder of HD Paranormal Simon, who catches me every time I fall...and fall I do.

I could continue the thanks and appreciation for another 100 pages I'm sure, but to those of you out there who have in some way contributed to this case, in however small a way, I thank you from the bottom of my heart.

~ Foreword ~

When Jayne asked me to write the Foreword for this book, I was thrilled and very excited to revisit the experience of meeting Peggy and Jayne for the first time. It was December 2016 and I had no knowledge of who or what I was going to meet. I had received a call from a rather anxious Zak Bagans saying he needed me to fly to Las Vegas to hold a séance with a haunted doll for his new TV show 'Deadly Possessions'. I have worked with Zak on several Ghost Adventures episodes as a psychic and medium, and he apparently knew that I was also a "doll person" and collector. For some reason this particular doll seemed to have extra importance and urgency to him, more than any other I'm aware of.

When I arrived in Las Vegas and was taken to my hotel, immediately strange things started happening. My brand-new cell phone went completely haywire. My brand-new tablet started mimicking it and also doing strange and never before seen oddities. My first thought was that it was technical aggravation due to some spirit not wanting me around. But, knowing your phone is your communication lifeline when filming, I knew I had to deal with it.

I proceeded to spend over four hours on the phone with my cell providers technical department. Going all the way to their top "expert" technicians and leaving them all dumbfounded one by one. So much so, that they literally overnighted me a new phone. (Almost unheard of with my provider!)

As the night wore on, I started realizing this was not just a faulty cell phone, Something far larger was at play here. I started sensing an ominous spirit hanging over me, a spirit that really didn't want me there. And, obviously I was not in a dark, scary haunted house – far from it – I was in an ultra- modern luxury high rise hotel on the Vegas strip, not the typical setting for the now overwhelming darkness I felt encompassing me.

I decided to watch some TV, but spirit had other plans. I would turn on the TV in the living room and then something would turn it off and turn on the TV in the bedroom or bathroom. I though "OK, fine I got it I'll take a shower instead!". I couldn't quite believe it when the shenanigans continued – as I stepped out of the shower the water came back on. I turned it off, it came back on! It happened a few times and by this point I was getting VERY excited as to what kind of doll I was going to meet the next day.

The next morning, I was picked up and taken to Zak Bagans newly created Haunted Museum. A sprawling 1930s era Tudor revival cottage. Not what you expect for find in downtown "Vegas", but perfectly befitting Zak and his haunted treasures! When I arrived tensions were already high. Zak excitedly showed me around some of his wonderful new displays – but was very careful NOT to tell me anything about the doll or just what we were doing – until we were actually on camera and filming. I must say, the crew really are extraordinarily good about that. They go to lengths to make sure everything is real, in the moment and not set up or planned. I was sequestered in a room with a mix of haunted items, paintings, cameras, filming equipment and a few curious spirits. My excitement was piqued by the time I was led in to film my first segment with Zak. There on camera he told me a tiny bit about Peggy the haunted doll, the ill effects she had on people and how he was truly concerned, even for viewers once the show went to air. The thickness of the energy had reached an all-time high by the time we went into the seance room and I met Jayne, one of the victims Katrin – and of course, Peggy. The focus of the séance was Katrin releasing the negative power that Peggy had over here. Her fear was seeming to feed it. Katrin was a rock star. She even let us leave her alone in the room with the doll for a few minutes. She faced her fears and won! During the séance, I tuned in to a beautiful female spirit inside Peggy. She was obviously not the entity giving people heart attacks and making them sick, that was something darker, deeper and more hidden. I got glimpses of it this darker spirit throughout the rest of the day. That is the spirit that sent flies to attack Zak and gave true physical harm to Katrin and so many others.

As all this was going on, I was also very aware of Jayne and her energy, strength, psychic awareness and power. I was glad. She has been a perfect guardian for Peggy the haunted doll. The girl spirit within Peggy is a bright light. The darker, more hidden spirit, just the opposite. Jayne has had quite an amazing and complicated task and a huge responsibility with this most amazing of dolls!

Enjoy the book and the journey. I know I will!

Patti

President

American Federation of Certified Psychics

& Mediums

(Voted #1 Psychic, Medium, Tarot Reader & Witch / Magical Practitioner in US in an International competition by Time Square Press 2016).

www.PattiNegri.com

~ Introduction ~

As a Paranormal Investigator I can honestly say that I have drifted back and forth between belief and skepticism over the past 18 years. I suppose that's inevitable when you set out to investigate something. Some days there will be evidence on one side of the fence, the next day quite the opposite. My skepticism has never been with regards to the afterlife itself I should point out. I absolutely believe that there is more to the existence of humanity than this mere physical body, and it's mechanical ability to perform rudimentary tasks. My belief in a higher purpose, that is, in the survival of the soul, is unwavering. Over the years though I have had doubts when it comes to the claims of others with regards to their experiences, and the perceived presence of ghosts and spirits. While I know for a fact that there will have been times in my career that I was deliberately misled by individuals claiming paranormal experiences, I am more inclined to believe that the majority of unreliable accounts come from those who have simply perceived explainable occurances in a supernatural way, themselves believing whole heartedly in what they are relaying. To put it bluntly, as the years pass I become more and more aware of man-kinds ability to fool himself and see what he wants to see. I am sure that this way of thinking came about for me following my introduction to the work of Harry Price early on in my interest. His rational explanations for perceived paranormal activity, and his exposition of fraudulent mediums absolutely planted the seed of doubt in my mind when it comes to this field. Sometimes the eyes do lie. I am also a generally pessimistic person and having witnessed first hand countless episodes of supposed paranormal occurrences taking place in peoples homes across the UK. I wouldn't say I have became passive when someone tells me they have lights flickering, or hear strange sounds however, but that my initial thought has changed from one of excitement as a 16 year old, to one of "ok it's probably nothing" as a 33 year old woman. Having said that, I am as passionate about making contact with the spirit world as ever. It is an obsession, a way of life. It is the flame of curiosity within me that cannot be extinguished. And so, I keep going.

I am incredibly fortunate that the person I chose to spend my life with is not only my Husband, but also my best friend, co- worker and confidant. Simon and I have travelled the length and breadth of this green island of ours visiting countless homes and helping those in need of support and answers. I can't claim that we have always been able to provide all of the answers, but we have certainly always given it our best shot. It has taken us to some fascinating places, both literally and spiritually. As our experience and knowledge organically grew and developed I reached a point where I felt that I had a comfortable, pretty well rounded understanding of what constitutes paranormal activity, the abilities and limitations of the spirit world, and what the living can come to expect when encountering such phenomena.

In September 2014 fate dealt us a hand that would prove me wrong. It turns out that I didn't have a well-rounded understanding of what spirits were truly capable of, and I hadn't experienced or studied every possible type of paranormal phenomena. The introduction of the doll we now call Peggy would lead me to question not only the untapped abilities of the human mind, but also the reality of existence as we perceive it, and the intricate layers that our souls may weave through on the journey to their ultimate resting place.

I am beginning to wonder whether time, space and communication are as linear as we perceive them to be. As you read this book, and learn of the experiences relating to this case, you too may begin to wonder whether there could well be more. Maybe in some telepathic way we all have the ability to communicate 4 dimensionally, not only back and forth with another living person using our voices and body language, but also, for want of a better description, diagonally through layers of time and space using conscious and sub- conscious thoughts and emotions, possibly through dreams. Dreams feature prominently in the case of Peggy. Those of you who have contacted me over the past year telling me of your dreams have all described your experiences in incredibly vivid detail. As if events were taking place in the physical 'conscious' world. In the 'awake' state. You have all described these dreams as being in some ways different to usual dreams. Sometimes they have been disturbing, sometimes sad or hopeful, but always incredibly memorable.

Of course I've heard of dream visitation before. As a child growing up I recall hearing a story from my Mother about the night her Father, my maternal Grandfather, passed away. She dreamt she was at a train station standing on the platform.

She could see everything in incredible detail, down to the clothes her father was wearing, the train itself and most of her surroundings. Her Father was a young man again, as she remembered him looking when she had been a child. He was saying goodbye to her and waving. She was crying and didn't want him to leave, but he told her he must, and asked her not to cry for he was happy.

The dream ended with her waving him off as he boarded a train and left.

When she woke the following morning she knew he had died. She got dressed and walked the 3 miles or so to her parents home. When she knocked the door my Grandmother opened the door in tears, but couldn't understand what my Mother was doing there or how she knew to come. My Grandfather had passed away in his sleep and to this day the family love to hear the story of how he visited my Mother to say his final farewell.

My Father too has been visited in his dreams. His own Father, my paternal Grandfather has apparently been coming forward since his passing in 1993. My Father describes him appearing through an egg shaped sphere of light, walking towards him.

They walk and talk for a while, he's gone and my father wakes up.

What is usually consistent with these types of dreams is that it is loved ones who are visiting us while our bodies are at rest. People we loved in life, and often they have a message of some kind. This is where the alleged dream visitations from Peggy are so intriguing, as these are people who have never even been in the same room as the doll let alone have any connection to the spirit, or spirits, that are connected to it.

So can those in the spirit world reach out to our subconscious? I believe it's possible. What I don't yet know, and maybe never will, is exactly how, and in Peggy's case, why.

Possibly the most worrying aspect of this case centres around the apparent ability this spirit (or energy) has to bring about physical, recordable reactions and effects in certain people. Of course to a degree we can put some instances down to suggestion, especially given that Peggy now has a degree of notoriety. People feeling uneasy staring at her eyes for example could easily be put down to the fact that they may have read about the experiences of Katrin Reedik, who famously suffered a heart attack during an automatic writing session we held with the doll. But it's not quite as simple as that.

Back in February 2015 when we first showed a photo of Peggy on our Facebook page, at that time just a doll with no name, she had no reputation, and no details or ideas about her were shared. In short, no one knew anything about her and yet scores of people were being affected in eerily similar ways by just seeing her image. None had read the experiences of the others. From just 1 photograph came a tidal wave of messages and emails within 24 hours, the details of which make it difficult to deny that something extraordinary was occurring.

What follows are just a few examples taken from those initial messages received via our website on 26th February.

Individual email addresses have not been included here for obvious privacy reasons.

26th February 2015 9:01am

Jayne, when you get a chance can you contact me please?

I've had a migraine and palpitations since seeing your doll.

J. Clare

9:14am

This doll you've just shown starts off my asthma! What's that about?! Don't like it.

R. Tromans

10:27am

I am not a psychic medium. Not even that sensitive really Jayne but I feel so very very sick and 'spinny' when I see that new doll of yours. I just think it's her energy do you feel it in person? At one point after I'd seen your photograph I was thinking about her eyes and I felt like the floor was moving like I was on a ship or something. Like travel sickness is the only way to describe it. Do you think it's an evil spirit or a demon here for a purpose? Hope you don't think I'm crazy but I'm sure it's not just me!

M. Taylor

11:05am

You should know that the doll you're working with now is having a strange affect on me. Since I saw the picture last night I have felt like someone is in my home off and on watching me. At around midnight last night I had her image on the monitor, when it started distorting and flickering. I then heard something like "shhh" before going cold down my left side. I had to turn the monitor off.

Dr S. Collins

11:15am

This is weird. Can dogs and cats sense evil? Since I opened the photo of that doll just my little terrier Molly has been snarling and growling at the screen. I'm a bit freaked.

J. Carlton

11.47am

NEW DOLL OMG! – Guys, I opened her photo and my dog started going crazy! Spinning in circles barking. I switched it off, he stopped, switched it on he started again! Now he's hiding and trembling. WTF!

F.Lead

My own personal goal in dealing with, and unraveling the mysterious case of Peggy the doll, remains around understanding how a spirit, the disembodied personality and energy of someone or something with intellectual ability, can apparently transfer feelings, emotions and physical pain through the layers of reality (space and time) upon a living person.

Is this a case of trans-dimensional telepathy or as some people believe, pure evil at work? Are we all in a sense, play- things with our lives in the hands of the undead?

Peggy doesn't like dogs. Well, at least that's one theory. There is certainly something unexplainable going on when it comes to canine companions.

They say that pets can sense evil, and maybe this is what we're dealing with but then my question would be why are cats, who are notoriously alerted to the presence of spirits via some sixth sense, not affected in the same way? That's not to say that we haven't had reports of cats reacting to her, as we have. But not to the degree that dogs seem to. A lady from Virginia contacted us recently to explain that each time she took an interest in Peggy, either looking at photographs or watching videos, she would have vivid dreams in which her cat was being chased by something unseen, which eventually caught the poor creature and choked it to death outside her front door. The reason the lady felt compelled to contact me was that 3 months after she first saw Peggy, and began having the dreams, she left the house one morning to find her cat dead at her feet and without being too graphic (as she unfortunately was with me!) it appeared quite clear that her cat *had* been strangled or choked to death by something or someone. So were the dreams at all related to Peggy? And if so, were they warnings of future tragedy or were they threats?

Several people have kindly agreed to let me share their stories in this book relating to their beloved pet dogs. I admit that a certain level of responsibility and guilt hangs over me for their suffering and loss. Dogs become part of our families and if it is true that whatever spirits are associated with this doll have in some way bought about negative and in some cases fatal reactions in anyone's beloved pet, then part of that remains with me.

The book will progress in chronological order as much as possible, with the odd reference to an earlier incident, and as it does so dear reader, I have every faith that like us, you will begin to realize that there comes a point when belief in mere coincidence or psychological suggestion cannot be sustained.

Chapter 1
~ The beginning ~

The morning of September 9th 2014 began like any other. With a 7-month-old baby and a 2.5 year old to feed, clean and dress, mornings were never easy. As always I stumbled from one mini crisis to the next until at 8am my Mother arrived to take over while I retreated to the office to check emails.

Juggling motherhood with my work continues to be a battle however as time goes on I do believe I'm winning...at least most days. Never let anyone tell you that working from home is easy!

So with my 2nd coffee of the day in my hand I sat down at the

laptop and logged on, my brain already on overdrive recalling all of the things I am yet to complete from the previous day. I scroll through social media messages then move onto the emails. I remember that unlike most mornings, when I can have anywhere between 10-30 new emails to sift through, I had just 1. I admit that a sense of relief washed over me as this meant I could focus on my current to do list, without adding more to it. Or so I thought. The subject simply read "Doll".

I knew from experience, and possibly instinct, that this would be a call for help, and it certainly was.

EXCERPT FROM EMAIL RECEIVED ON 09:09:14

"Dear Sir/Madam,

I am writing this is the hope that you can please help me. I have reached a point now at which I can't carry on this way. Let me just explain that I have always had a huge belief in the paranormal and the idea that spirits are all around us. I didn't know though that they could affect the living in the way they have been affecting me. I can't talk to anyone about this, as I am sure they will think I am crazy. Some days I wonder if I'm crazy myself. I have a doll here which I am sure is causing my house, maybe even me, to be haunted. If I hadn't lived through it for the last few months I'd think that sounded completely insane.

I read that you have a lot of experience so please reply and tell me what I should do. The doll is no longer in my house and I won't have it here. I can't sleep at all and today is now the 5th day that I have been awake, no sleep at all.

There is a figure that comes to me at night, stands at my bed. Its dark, a lady I think, but doesn't move or speak. I end up frozen to the bed in fear. I tried to put a cross on my wall and pray to Jesus but it doesn't help.

Please come soon J.W"

For the purposes of protecting her identity I will refer to the sender, the previous owner of Peggy, as J.W throughout this book.

The email was considerably longer than this, and it was clear from the way it progressed that this was a person who was on the edge of their sanity, but had only very recently found herself there. Of course, we had to go.

As you might expect HD Paranormal have a set procedure in place when a call for help or guidance comes in. My Husband Simon and I together with Hazel Myers, a local psychic we have worked with on numerous cases, spend time going over the content of the email or message, going backwards and forwards with the sender to ask various questions before agreeing to a visit, however in this case, something told me instinctively that for this person, time was of the essence and that we needed to act fast. I didn't yet know what exactly we would be encountering of course, but as Simon later described it "this was one that chose us" and so we had no option.

Without consulting either Simon or Hazel I replied asking for an address, and saying we would be there later that week.

Looking back I felt driven to act quickly and not hesitate. It was very impulsive.

A few days later we found ourselves on the M5 motorway heading north to Sheffield from Stourbridge. I recall an air of tension amongst the passengers and Hazel in particular was very quiet in the car throughout the journey. It wasn't too surprising as she often goes into 'the zone' as she calls it when trying to connect with the spirit world, however there seemed to be something bothering her, and her unease was apparent, something I didn't recognize as part of her usual demeanor. She later shared with us that at some point in the journey she had closed her eyes and asked for some protection and support in the upcoming encounter, something she does frequently. Instead of the usual circle of golden light she expected to feel surround her, she saw something quite different.

"I remember that the car journey was particularly uncomfortable that day. It is only a 90 minute or so drive but I felt almost trapped in time. When I asked my guides to surround me with light and protection the face of a man appeared to me and whispered 3 words to me. "they won't help". I was shaken but didn't want to worry Jayne or Si so I just carried on staring out of the window, at trees, signposts anything I could in an attempt to distract myself.

I knew we were driving towards something that would challenge us, and part of me was screaming inside to turn around and go home".

Hazel Myers, Psychic Medium.

Unaware of the level of discomfort Hazel was experiencing, Simon and I were chatting away about the email, going over and over the things we'd been told and joking that if it were genuine then the sender was in a real life horror movie! (It is with an undeniable discomfort that I now recall our joke).

JW had described footsteps on the landing outside her bedroom, a figure at the end of the bed, waking at 3am each night, scratching sounds from within the walls the list went on. We both agreed that this would be an interesting experience if it turned out to be true! At just after 3pm, anxious and intrigued, we pulled up outside a modest semi-detached house in a quiet cul-de-sac. There were pink roses to the left of the front door, a small gnome holding a welcome sign by the cast iron gate and the overall impression was one of order, happiness and contentment. This appeared to be the home of someone who took pride in its appearance but the closed curtains and collection of unopened milk bottles on the doorstep hinted that something had been affecting the usual rhythm of things. As we got out of the car and began approaching the gate there was a degree of curtain twitching from the adjoining house and something told me that they were not the only ones in the immediate area to be curious about our arrival. The rebellious streak in me always wants to give them something to look at when this happens but I've learned to accept that it is human nature to be curious – in fact without curiosity I wouldn't be doing what I'm doing.

After knocking a few times, an exhausted looking woman slowly opened the door and uttered 2 exasperated words "about time".

Having had 2 children in the space of 2 years myself, I know only too well the levels of fatigue a person can still function under and I would describe her overall appearance as that of a woman who has been physically, mentally and emotionally drained of every last ounce of energy. I could tell that her comment about sleepless nights had not been an exaggeration. I introduced everyone and naturally took a step towards entering the house. The door moved quickly back towards me leaving just a small gap, enough to still see half of the occupants face. "not in here yet" was all she said. I turned to Simon, and with the intuitive understanding between Husband and Wife, I knew what he was thinking. Simon is more skeptical than I, and in that moment I knew he thought she may be unhinged and was now on 'red alert' for more unusual, potentially dangerous behaviour.

I knew this wouldn't be an easy process but my years spent as a Mental Health Specialist equipped me with the ability to engage unwilling individuals, and reach out to them and eventually prove worthy of their trust. In short I'm a pretty good listener and it was a skill that would be my most invaluable tool here.

"How can we help you?" I asked, feeling this was the best way to handle her reluctance to let us in.

"It's out here" she replied stepping out of the house and pointing around the corner to a side gate. From her email I recalled that she wouldn't have the doll in the house and I realised that my curiosity about just where she kept the doll was about to be satisfied. As we were led to a small red brick outbuilding I began to feel apprehensive. If there was a time to change our minds it was now.

Hazel must have felt the same as she too was walking uncharacteristically slowly.

Simon in typical fashion led the way maintaining his very matter of fact demeanor, something I am repeatedly grateful for as he keeps us grounded.

Once we reached the small door of the building there was an awkward silence for a few moments while an unspoken decision over who should go in and get the doll was being made. Hazel took the first step towards the building and entered. More or less as soon as she was inside and out of sight, she was back out again. One hand was on her brow the other was reaching out for somewhere to sit down. A large plant pot nearby acted as her support as she steadied herself. After about 20 seconds she explained that she felt quite nauseous and was light headed. She assured us she was ok but asked that I go in to retrieve the doll as she felt she had 'opened up' too much psychically too soon. Thinking back to that day, and the first encounter with the doll, Hazel seemed very different to us. She was usually so calm and in control but this day was unusual and as the weeks and months ahead of us would prove, there was quite a good reason for it.

Quite nervously I went inside and taking a moment for my eyes to adjust to the darkness I began looking around for a doll. In my minds eye I had imagined your average sized doll, possibly porcelain and rather dusty. I couldn't see one.

Old paint tins with the lids not quite on properly, paint brushes solid with hardened varnish, a bucket, a stack of logs, cobwebs, a few sun loungers, just an ordinary garden shed. Looking back I'm amazed at how clearly I can still recall this particular day, and how fresh the images are in my mind. I guess that's what happens in life when something that alters you forever happens. After several moments I noticed a roll of what looked like carpet on the floor, which later turned out to be a thick red blanket. I lifted it up and carried it outside. JW exhaled slowly and loudly in the way you might do if you are feeling incredibly sick having stood up too quickly. Simon reached for the red bundle expecting it to be heavy and was surprised by how light it was. I slowly unrolled the top of the mysterious package to reveal blonde hair, then blue eyes and finally a face. I looked at JW who was now trembling and holding her hand over her mouth as if desperate to suppress a scream or cry. I had never witnessed such overwhelming fear towards an object before, although since owning Peggy, I have grown accustomed to the reactions of those she has affected. It was at this moment that I had a curious experience, which was to become the first of many whilst in the presence of Peggy the doll. My ears began ringing, then buzzing, as if I had an inner radio transmitter which was struggling to pick up any recognizable frequency. It felt like a combination of realization and panic. My head began to feel numb as the ringing increased in pitch. It lasted maybe 60 seconds, but felt like much longer.

Hazel put an arm around JW and led her back towards the house while Simon took the doll, still largely covered, into the car before returning. This time we were granted access to the house and sat for around 90 minutes listening in fascination, to the experiences this doll has allegedly been creating.

I took notes, we asked questions occasionally and once we felt we had as much information as she could give us, we said our goodbyes. Upon leaving the house, I asked JW my usual parting question, "shall I keep you updated?"

Her response left no room for confusion when she said:

"That doll nearly ruined my life. I want to forget it ever existed and I hope God protects you all".

Chapter 2
~ My Illness ~

Usually once a new object arrives back at the research area, we begin immediately. We clear a dedicated space for the doll or object and run some baseline tests to establish if there are any draughts, points of electrical fluctuation and so on. Once completed we attempt to isolate the object (usually in our sealed glass cabinet) followed by the setting up of night vision cameras, digital cameras, motion detectors, temperature gauges, EMF meters, trigger objects...you name it, we try it. All with a view to experiencing, but more importantly, capturing something interesting. Something we can then use as a foundation for future studies. I am not too comfortable with the word 'experiments' when it comes to connection and communication with those in the spirit world. Given that spirits are essentially human in their thought processes and emotional responses, it seems almost cruel and immoral to experiment as such. A more appropriate way of looking at it therefore is to focus on testing the environment – the scientifically measurable reactions and changes in a localized area - in and around a specific object, rather than expecting to make contact with or gain evidence of an actual person in spirit, at least in these early stages.

Things were rather different with Peggy however. She was indeed placed in a secure spot, isolated and with various pieces of gadgetry to keep her company in those first few months, but what was different, and looking back I can think of no good reason for it, was that we didn't attempt any kind of contact with a potential spirit. Maybe it was apprehension.

Initial EMF readings had proved inconclusive and there had been nothing clear on either night vision or audio recordings, so naturally after a few weeks our usual next step should have been to conduct a series of séances. Hazel too seemed to be in no hurry to investigate or form a connection. Little did we know at that time that someone or something connected with the doll, as it later became clear, was becoming increasingly frustrated at being ignored.

In November 2015, roughly 6 weeks after we bought the doll home with us, I began to suffer with incredibly debilitating fatigue, to the point at which after 2 weeks of migraines, nausea and dizziness, I was unable to get out of bed, and if I did make it down the stairs, I made it no further than the sofa. For the first week or so I recall Simon and I put it down to our hectic lifestyle, small children and so on but as time went on and I became worse not better, despite sleeping solidly for 8 or 9 hours a night and we began to worry. Especially when 3 independent doctors couldn't give me an explanation either. Blood tests showed normal levels of thyroxin and so thyroid issues were ruled out, I had no signs of anemia or other illnesses. I didn't want to believe that 'the doll' as she was then known could be the cause, but I kept hearing JW's words over and over in my head and I knew that what I was experiencing was exactly what she had described in her early days with the doll. Hazel suggested that she remove the doll for a week or two, to really test the theory, but before agreeing, I wanted an independent opinion. I'd heard of a local Medium and Clairvoyant named Patricia Redmonn, with a wonderful reputation amongst her clients, and booked an appointment under a false name. It felt misleading, but I wanted to make sure that she couldn't do her research beforehand, having fallen victim to a number of fraudulent psychic mediums over the years. I wasn't sure if I would be well enough to make it out to see her but I knew I would try my best. On November 5th at 2.45pm, mustering all of my strength and conviction, I put the doll in the car and drove the short journey to Patricia's Well-being Centre. As I approached the large black wrought-iron double gates I suddenly felt nervous. What if she thought I was crazy? I had to risk it. If she did I would never have to see her again anyway so figured I had nothing to lose. I parked next to the building, a beautiful large Georgian place with tall sash windows and an imposing black front door with brass knocker. I decided to leave the doll in the car for the time being, as I hadn't mentioned bringing an object along and so thought I would test the water with Patricia first, maybe gauging whether or not she was able to pick up on my reasons for visiting her. I entered the reception area and was greeted by a lovely young girl who asked me to take a seat. As everyone knows when you're in a waiting area, a minute can seem like an hour. I found myself picking up magazines and flicking through them, without actually taking in any of the information on the pages. Just mindlessly scanning each while all the time just wishing my name would be called to put me out of my misery. I'm not the most patient person in the world, and being kept waiting is something I loathe. Eventually I was asked to follow the receptionist down a long corridor towards the rear of the building and was shown into a small room where Patricia was sitting at a round table smiling at me, and waving her hand for me to sit opposite her. After the pleasantries she said "your friends can come in too if you like". My brow furrowed and with a puzzled look I enquired as to her meaning.

"Oh I saw you arrive, your friends might be cold sitting in the car. Just a thought". She said casually.

"er...I'm here alone" I said, slightly embarrassed for her that she had mistaken me for someone else arriving.

"You're in the black 4x4 aren't you?" she asked.

"Yes that's right, but..." before I could finish Patricia spoke again.

"Wasn't there a man and a woman with you when you pulled up?" she enquired.

There was a brief look of acknowledgment between us before I spoke, and in that moment I knew she was aware that she has misread the situation. The figures she had seen sitting in the car with me, were in spirit.

"No, no-one came with me...that I know of anyway!" I nervously laughed.

I expected Patricia to begin the reading, but instead, a new feeling had taken hold of both of us. It was uneasy. Suddenly Patricia stood up and stepped back from the table. Holding the left side of her head she apologized and walked towards a window at the far end of the room. I knew she was looking for my car, maybe to check that I wasn't lying, maybe in anticipation of seeing the 2 spirit people again, I'm not sure, but what happened next was quite unexpected.

"I'm sorry sweetheart, I can't read for you today. I've got a terrible headache starting up, the energy is quite heavy in the room. If you speak to Valerie on the front desk she'll sort your refund out for you". I could tell that she was in somewhat of a hurry for me to leave, which unnerved me a little. Not wanting to make an awkward situation worse, I promptly made my way towards the door, and with a final backwards glance I noticed Patricia had her head down with her eyes closed and was whispering. I said nothing more and with a sigh of disappointment I left. The girl at the reception desk, whom I now knew was named Valerie looked surprised to see me already.

"She can't read for me apparently, and told me to come for a refund?" I said uncomfortably. Valerie was very professional and with a quick "Oh, ok no problem" she shuffled some papers, before opening a drawer and handing me my money. "See you soon" she said casually as I walked out.

"I doubt it" I replied under my breath.

The experience had left me with so many unanswered questions. Who had Patricia seen with me that day? Why did they make her feel so uncomfortable, to the point of wanting me to leave? Feeling lost and perplexed I felt I had no real option but to take Hazel up on her offer of looking after Peggy for me for a while in the hope that I would begin to feel better. On November 13th Hazel took Peggy with her and it took just 4 days for me to feel normal. Suddenly I could concentrate properly again, I wasn't constantly yawning and my skin, which had taken on a greyish tone and was increasingly dry, began to appear healthy once more. The only way I can really describe what I experienced was in likening it to a battery. I felt that my energy was literally being drained from me with such force, that no amount of rest could recharge me. I later read that this phenomenon is often referred to as Psychic Drain or Psychic Attack and it is believed that some spirits do indeed drain and make use of the energy of the living. It's not always intentional and often when groups are out on ghost hunts, someone will feel unwell, dizzy and maybe nauseous. This can all be associated with the atmospheric changes in an area where there are ghosts or spirits present. In cases where a conscious spirit deliberately does this however, it is usually to make themselves known in some way, either by moving objects, making lights flicker or possibly appearing as an apparition. Many professional investigators and psychic mediums believe that feeling drained of energy is the primary symptom associated with prolonged spirit presence.

Put simply, spirits need to plug into someone else's energy, which drains the host. An analogy is that a living person with an earthbound spirit attachment is riding a bicycle up a hill and carrying a hitchhiker on the back of the bike who has no pedals to help push! That's certainly how I felt. Every movement, every effort was tiring.

After 3 weeks of continual improvement I felt that it was time for Peggy to return to us, but not before Hazel cast psychic protection around my family and I in an attempt to prevent a reoccurrence and to this day, it continues to work.

Chapter 3
~ The doll goes public ~

As previously mentioned, February 2015 marked the beginning of public interest in Peggy. It's not uncommon, in the early stages of any investigation, for us to update social media followers on cases we're working on. This can include sharing photographs, providing new evidence or discussing theories on various elements of the paranormal. Given the experiences Peggy's previous owner had described however, twinned with my subsequent and apparently connected illness in November 2014, we held fire on sharing this new potentially haunted object with the world. The decision to do so was never really consciously agreed upon or discussed. It simply happened. The period from September 2014 to January 2015 seemed to pass in a blur, almost like a dream with occasional flickers of the nightmarish. Things were different in our home. There was a great deal of unrest and admittedly unhappiness too. Looking back, our family and even those few colleagues we had shared Peggy with, were not quite themselves that Christmas and New Year. Something had changed in us all and the regular order of things had become fragmented, but at that time of course we couldn't see it let alone recognize or discuss it. Our home became unsettled and looking back we are aware of how Simon and I didn't want to be in the house very much at all, in fact we spent very little time together at all for a while as if a wedge was being slowly driven between us. It was subtle, unidentifiable and gradual. I've done a great deal of reading since on the theories around the abilities of supernatural beings to affect our relationships, however cases and ideas always seem to centre around demonic entities. It's well documented that darker forces enjoy human suffering and if you believe in that kind of thing, it's quite easy to see how part of their grand design would be to wreak havoc, destroy relationships and in turn destroy our happiness. In raising this point, I am in no way claiming that I know there to be a demonic entity attached to Peggy, in fact it' not something I would ever say lightly, however as time goes on I can't be absolutely sure beyond doubt that there is not.

Towards the latter part of January 2015, as my health returned to normal and the overall mood in our home seemed to be lifting, we decided to focus our attentions on Peggy, and try to, for want of a better phrase, work her out.

When we took that first photograph on 25th February I remember feeling a sense of relief. Almost as if this doll, then with no name of course, had held some kind of power over us all since it came into our lives. There was now a secret guest in our home, quietly manipulating our behavior, our feelings and draining our energy. It sounds far fetched granted but when casting my mind back to that specific period in our lives, it is the only way I can accurately, at least accurately to my mind, describe what was going on from my point of view.

And so, the photograph that signaled the true beginning of our journey with Peggy was shared on our website. Before I go on to describe what subsequently ensued I feel it important to set the scene and give an idea of what constituted, at that time, a 'standard' level of communication from visitors to the aforementioned website. Trawling back through contact forms submitted for the period of March 2014 to May 2014 as an example, just 36 submissions can be noted. These cover all topics from requests for help to spam. So on average, prior to the introduction of Peggy, we received roughly 12 messages a month via the website. As is the case today, people generally tend to contact us through social media or via direct email rather than our websites contact page.

The photograph of Peggy posted onto our website on 25th February led to over 60 individual messages being submitted in the first 24 hours, with a further 37 over the next 24 hours. Simon and I sat together scrolling through them with concern. Each time we saw the same words repeated by different people my stomach felt knotted and everything I thought I knew about ghosts, spirits and the afterlife seemed to spiral from my reach. If these people were to be believed, then there was absolutely something undeniable going on in relation to this doll, and not only that, but it was strong enough to bring about physical effects in someone without that person being present. We needed to look at this objectively. Could these people simply be wide open to suggestion or mass hysteria? None of the submissions were visible to anyone but us as our contact form submissions are confidential and do not appear publically on the website, and so the idea of someone reading someone else's experience, and suddenly believing it was happening to them too could be ruled out. Was it a prank?

Maybe a few friends got together and created fake email accounts to mock our work and waste our time? That would be possible if we hadn't gone on to contact everyone individually to confirm and discuss these experiences along with checking their locations tied up. These were people from all walks of life from all over the world. It seemed highly improbable that this was a mass prank even back then. Now with further experiences seeming to confirm what those early messages suggested, we know these people were genuine.

Two things were clear to Simon and I by 28th February 2015.

1. People felt strongly enough about seeing the following photograph to get in touch with us immediately when previously we had received minimal contact through our website.
2. We were going to need help with this case.

The photograph, originally published 25th February 2015

Chapter 4
~ Hazel Myers ~

Anyone who has followed the work of HD Paranormal will be familiar with the name Hazel Myers. It is Hazel who we came to reply upon more than anyone as our experiences and investigations developed over a period of 17 years. Hazel is an incredibly gifted, straight talking psychic medium. She pulls no punches and isn't afraid of telling you things you don't necessarily want to hear. She is always honest, and if she feels she can't help us, then she doesn't. I've lost count of the amount of individuals I've met at my local Spiritualist Church over the years, who after hearing abut the line of work we're in, were suddenly gifted with psychic abilities themselves and were offering to join us on visits and investigations.

What interested me about Hazel, from the very first time I met her, was that she didn't seem to care much for her gift. At times I am sure she feels it a burden, then there are times when it gives her a way of bringing comfort to the bereaved, but in all cases, however she feels about it at the time or whoever she is with, it is never something she likes to shout or make a fuss about. It is part of her, in the same way she can draw incredible landscapes (just one of her many talents). I believe Hazel Myers makes wonderful connections to the spirit world.

It's effortless and natural. To coin a cliché, it's a gift.

We learned early on in our dealings with Hazel that she suffers from several social anxieties, and in writing this book I have her permission to disclose certain facts, for which I would like to extend my gratitude.

She hates crowds, dislikes socializing generally and has a fear of being photographed. The latter is quite intriguing for me from a psychological point of view, (although I am forever trying not to psycho-analyse people these days!) and I have at one time or another tried to understand where this stems from.

Is it a fear of her soul being affected or stolen in some way, as was the belief of the early Victorians, or is it more a self esteem issue relating to her appearance. I am yet to unravel this mystery, and knowing Hazel the way I do, I doubt I ever shall, and so we accept it as one of her quirks.

Before inviting Hazel to accompany us on an investigation in 2006, our first with her, I remember asking her to provide me with a reading. I didn't mind if she preferred to use cards, palmistry, tea leaves or even a crystal ball! But I wanted to feel confident that there was at least something to her abilities.

Something I could believe in. That afternoon is as fresh I my mind as if it were yesterday.

I was asked to visit Hazel at her home which she shares with 6 cats, 2 tortoises and a parot named Clive, which to this day I find quite amusing. Her home is a modest ex-local authority 3 bed semi with the most wonderfully welcoming atmosphere.

As I stepped through the door I felt I had been there before and was instantly at home. Far from being a mystical place of incense and dream catchers, Hazels home is very 'mumsy'. She loves drawing and painting, and has a weakness for Catherine Cookson novels. Every inch of her sideboards and shelving is covered in an array of mismatched photo frames displaying her children and grandchildren and the overall feeling you get when you walk in there is one of genuine warmth and love. A pot of tea and 3 shortbread biscuits later we were sitting in her conservatory gazing out of the window. I had been there about 45 minutes and was beginning to wonder if she was putting me off, when suddenly she said something quite out of the blue.

"you know you haven't lost that gold ring". I stared at her. This was the moment, and it had arrived sooner that I'd expected in her reading, if this was her reading! Mentioning something as general as a missing ring to someone is a trick used by many cold readers to draw further information from a sitter. Also, it's very probable that a good proportion of people, have at some point lost a ring or (as some psychics then go on to say once you tell them you've never lost a ring) KNOW someone who has.

"Ring?" I asked.

"You had a gold ring, I can see it. Unusual it is, with black stones all around it in the shape of flowers. You thought you'd lost it a few years ago but you haven't, It's about somewhere". I was gob-smacked. Of course I believe in the supernatural and have been given what I believe to be genuine messages from the spirit world through psychic mediums and clairvoyants in the past, but this was so sudden, so natural and so accurate that it was as if she could see right into my mind. I'd been given a ring when I was 18 fitting the description exactly. It was 18ct gold with black stones in the shape of flowers. I haven't seen it for years and quite some time ago I assumed it to be lost forever.

I am always very careful not to give too much away in these types of situations, being only too familiar with techniques like 'Cold reading' or 'Shot-gunning' in which the reader will make very generalized statements and read the sitters responses to form the next part of their reading. Some psychics are very good at using these techniques and I have been fooled by a couple myself when meeting them for the first time. This was not the case here. Not once had Hazel told me she saw someone connected to me who passed from a problem with their heart or chest. Nor had she said "Who's John? I've got a John coming through".

No in fact I was quite unaware that she was receiving images, messages and information as we sat side my side. As I was about to respond telling her that she was right, and that I had loved that gold ring, she spoke first.

"you haven't got to say anything love, I can see it, and I can see that little mother of pearl box you keep all your other rings in. Very nice that is". Well that was it.

I was blown away. In the days that followed I tried, as I do with most things, to debunk Hazel. I scrolled through my Facebook photos to see if I'd ever taken a photo in my bedroom showing that mother of pearl box, but I knew deep down I hadn't. Hazel hadn't researched anything. She was gaining her information from an altogether different source.

10 years later I still reach out to Hazel when I feel we need clarity or deeper understanding, and it is Hazel who we have to thank for some our most memorable and enlightening experiences in terms of spirit communication. The past 18 months have however seen a decline in Hazels health, and it cannot be ignored that this coincides with the introduction of Peggy into our lives. Hazel has had something of a

rollercoaster ride with this case. Initially, as previously mentioned, she suffered bouts of nausea and dizziness.

During later séances we've witnessed her energy deplete significantly while in direct contact with the spirit or spirits connected to the doll, and each time a session is over, she seems to take longer to regain her strength. And yet she battles on, determined to help us understand exactly what we're dealing with. We have on the flip side had some wonderfully motivating breakthroughs also when studying Peggy with Hazels help. Had it not been for Hazel, we may never have known there was a spirit by the name of Peggy at all, although we did later receive the same name from a second psychic named Chris based in Wales, it had been given to us initially by Hazel along with the name Margaret, for which Peggy is often used as a nickname. Hazel and Chris do not know each other, Hazel has no social media involvement or interest, and so Chris's information, quite out of the blue in February 2015 confirmed the name as important.

The day will come, and I fear not too far from now, where I have to call an end to her involvement in our work, for her own sake. She once explained to me that being able to connect with those who have passed into spirit is incredibly demanding.

"There is always someone wanting your attention, whether on this side of life or the other". She described it as being like a telephone exchange. "Calls are coming in from all directions, they meet in the middle and although I can hear them all I can only direct one at a time, meaning that someone somewhere is always disappointed or angry".

In the 17 or 18 years I've had an interest in Spiritualism I can say hand on heart I believe I have only encountered a handful of truly gifted individuals who have the ability to communicate with the dead. I am honored to call Hazel my friend.

Chapter 5
~ Religion ~

As a Catholic, although admittedly not a devout or even practising one, I do hold firm belief in the overall power of good over evil and of the absolute need for religious intervention when dealing with darker forces i.e. Demons. I'm not sure exactly what I believe that 'good' to be however, in that I can't say with any degree of certainty that I believe there is a God. I'm not convinced by the story of Adam and Eve and there are too many holes in the creation story, especially in light of scientific discoveries in relation to the universe. But I don't think science and religion need to be enemies, or even viewed as independent from each other.

Maybe it's that good old generational Catholic superstition that leads me to have a set of rosary beads, bought home from The Vatican in 2009 and anointed in Holy water monthly, hanging on my bedroom mirror. Maybe that's also why I keep a supply of bottled Holy water in my home 'just incase'. It could also be superstition that led me to place a set of rosary beads around the neck of Peggy before we began studying her at length. Some part of me definitely felt that in doing so I was openly asking for help from a higher power. Asking for protection from darkness. At no point in introducing religious paraphernalia into the investigation was I trying to provoke or entice something into demonstrating their frustration or repulsion, in fact I can say with conviction that the thought there may be something Demonic present never entered my consciousness. It rarely does truth be told. I believe in dark forces, but I also believe them to be incredibly rare and quite obvious in their behaviour and motivation. There is nothing subtle about the psychological or physical attack of a Demon. We felt that whatever was going on with Peggy was prolonged, patient and steady, but that's not to say that we weren't going to encounter difficulties with regards to religion.

The image in Chapter 3 shows Peggy wearing a cross. Of the 60+ comments that came in on 25th February 2015, almost half of them, 28 to be exact, mentioned a need to remove it. Some claimed they were hearing a voice telling them that the spirit hated the symbol of the cross, a few had dreams indicating that the sign of the cross would provoke negative reactions, others simply said they had a strong gut feeling that the cross should be removed.

Of course there will always be a number of people who will focus on the religious aspect of any case, and the wearing of a cross may be seen by some as a sign of provocation more than protection – how many possession based horror movies depict the lead characters as religious, their home littered with images of the Virgin Mary and a cross hanging above their bed? Quite a few if you think about it. Part of me has always believed that in adorning ones home with such artifacts could potentially act as a "red rag to a bull" (I'm aware that this is a myth, as Bulls are simply agitated by the movement of the fabric not its colour but the meaning behind the phrase stands) – it could well be that those who demonstrate a strong religious persuasion are the ultimate prize for a Demon, and that religious symbology could be more of a catalyst than a deterrent.

However, as already mentioned, at the time of placing the rosary upon the doll none of these thoughts or concerns passed through my mind.

Amongst the initial messages were mentions of possible Jewish connections. Some people felt a link with the Holocaust, and while this is still an area we're yet to delve into and research at length, we cannot deny that it seems uncanny for complete strangers, each without knowledge of the others statements, to mention such a thing. Some also suggested using a Star of David as a trigger object. In addition we had a notable number of messages mentioning a fear or hatred of institutions.

Keen to keep an open mind, and try any methods of divination possible, we decided that with the help of Hazel, we would hold an automatic writing session, with the doll present. Maybe nothing would happen, or maybe, as I've experienced twice before, some words or sentences may come through. I don't participate in these sessions myself, at least I do not hold the pencil. I am always an observer. Hazel being highly experienced in most forms of divination and spirit communication enters a trance and acts as a conduit for the writings.

The date was set for 16th March and prior to the session I thought it might be interesting to film a short clip explaining to our social media followers what we were about to do. I'm not exactly sure what prompted me to do this, but sometimes these thoughts come to us and for better or worse we often go ahead with them! So we filmed a short clip whilst driving to Hazels.

I uploaded it to Facebook immediately and by the time I got to Hazels home I had received a message from a lady in Glasgow named Katrin Reedik. *(this was the beginning of a relationship with Katrin that would lead us to very unexpected places both physically and mentally)*.

This was the message:

Katrin Reedik   3/16, 12:23pm
Hi. Whats going on with Peggy? My heart is racing so fast and I feel dizzy

Im in pain

Katrin Reedik   3/16, 12:30pm
After i saw your post it vanished from site and my phone went crazy.

Jayne Harris   3/16, 12:31pm
I know the first vanished??

Katrin Reedik   3/16, 12:31pm
Yes

Jayne Harris   3/16, 12:31pm
She is affecting people currently. I'm trying to get to the bottom of it all

Katrin Reedik   3/16, 12:32pm
My heart is like racing horse

It was true that my initial upload had unexpectedly disappeared from the page a few moments after being posted, but this could easily be chalked up to a technical glitch, and so I didn't think too much of it. Katrin was clearly feeling uncomfortable and so I advised her to take a break for the computer.

At this point we had arrived with Hazel and shortly after receiving these messages, at roughly 12.45pm, the automatic writing session began. Peggy was placed in a small chair next to Hazels fireplace, and Hazel sat at a small desk next to the window. As always in these situations the room was dimly lit with candles, with just the slightest slither of sunlight passing through the closed curtains illuminating the desk. Before entering her trance, Hazel mentioned to me that she felt something was going to happen.

"We're provoking something today I think" she said with her eyes closed.

"What do you mean?" I asked.

"I don't know yet. I just feel like something's about to happen".

In the past Hazel has described these sensations to me, as not unlike the feeling you get sometimes before a storm. A heaviness in the air, a pressure that is all around you, and she wasn't wrong. Things did indeed occur which we cannot explain. Not only in terms of the writing itself, which did provide us with several groups of words, which we later wrote out neatly for future reference. What I believe Hazel had been sensing, and what I only discovered the following day was that in the 1-hour window in which we were asking Peggy (or any spirits present) for a sign, Katrin Reedik suffered a heart attack. This was too severe to ignore. Of course simple coincidence will always be one explanation. But one can't escape the fact that another explanation, and a terrifying one at that, is that Katrin was directly targeted by someone or something present around this doll, something which was aware of her interest in the case and the fact that Katrin was psychologically present – with us in thought – during the session.

Now this begs several questions: Does the spirit world function through a form of telepathy? Are we all part of some greater cosmic energy field, with information and communication buzzing around within it, transmitted from each and every one of us, whether living or deceased?

Can spirits even cause physical reactions as powerful as heart attacks?

I'd say there's every chance that psychologically someone could find themselves experiencing problems like this connected to extreme shock. Maybe the sight of a ghost standing directly in front of someone could potentially shock them to such a degree that a heart attack may follow. However in the case of Katrin Reedik there was no fear factor. She wasn't with Peggy, she wasn't in a spooky location and so the psychological explanation is largely irrelevant here, although can't be completely ruled out at least as a contributory factor. Katrin herself believes firmly that in opening her mind up to Peggy during that 1-hour window she somehow made herself spiritually, and consequently physically vulnerable.

Understandably as a result of her experience, Katrin became cautious of Peggy choosing to avoid photographs and images of her online for quite some time incase she suffered further reactions. The true extent of her fear was revealed and addressed in December 2015 when Katrin agreed to come face to face with Peggy, with surprising results...but that's for another chapter.

Katrin Reedik

Needless to say, the attack on Katrin coupled with ongoing messages advising us to remove the cross as it was provoking an "angry demon" had left us questioning the nature of this phenomena and the potential entity we were dealing with. If there was some form of paranormal connection here, was it human? Was it evil?

Curious to test the water in terms of religion I consulted with a Spiritualist Church, 'Light of the Spirit' in the West Midlands, where I met for the first time with Reverend Martin Jenkins.

Martin is a kind man, and never rubbishes any idea or theory when it comes to the spirit world. Having had a premonition himself in 1992 in which he foresaw the death of his wife in vivid detail, which subsequently came to pass, he is a man with a very open mind and strong belief in the supernatural. After speaking at length about not only this case, but also our other previous experiences, he agreed that we could conduct a group gathering (he wasn't keen on the term séance) at the church on March 30th 2015. We decided to request that he be

present along with an independent note taker Donna Griffiths who had been a member at the church herself for several years, but who until the evening of the gathering, Simon and I had never met. Hazel led the gathering and the room was arranged as shown on the following page.

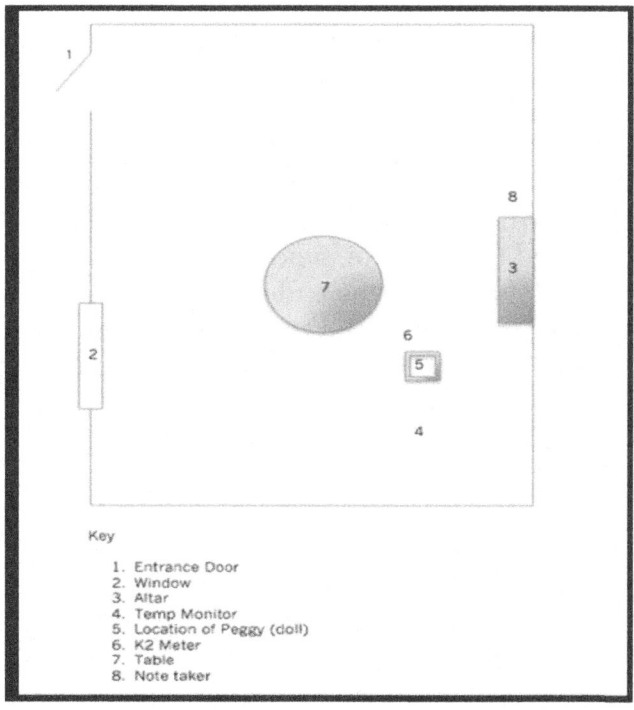

Key

1. Entrance Door
2. Window
3. Altar
4. Temp Monitor
5. Location of Peggy (doll)
6. K2 Meter
7. Table
8. Note taker

Personally I felt an extreme sense of calm entering this space. Psychologically I felt that simply by being in the church, we had some form of protection or support around us – that ingrained Catholicism again no doubt.

It was very comforting and I felt, at that stage prepared. Little did I know that what I would experience that evening would be something I was not at all prepared for and an experience which would be relived in my dreams many times over the ensuing months.

We greeted each other and, in that way you do when in the company of people you don't know very well, we made polite conversation. Looking back it seems bizarre. There we were about to embark upon potential communication with the spirit world, via a large 1960s plastic doll but all we could think to say to each other was how cold it had been! I guess there is no template for how to behave in such a situation. Everyone took their respective places and waited. I was the last to be seated, being responsible for placing Peggy in her position close to the small altar (fig.5). We had decided that Donna, who would act as not only our note taker, but eyes and ears should we miss anything going on around the room, should sit away from the main table and so had positioned a chair on the opposite side of the altar to Peggy. A *K2 EMF meter was placed next to Peggy and we began.

*EMF meters are frequently used by paranormal investigators to detect changes in the electro-magnetic field in a given situation, which is believed by some to indicate the presence of a ghost or spirit.

Investigative notes:

group session held with Doll - Peggy

Date: 30:03:15

Time: 11.20pm start

Duration: Approx 1hour

Present:

Jayne Harris, Simon Harris, Hazel Myers, Donna Griffiths

Martin Jenkins (Pastor)

Temp: 18 degrees

11.20pm:

MJ recites the blessing and the 4 team members around the table join hands. HM takes over and requests that Peggy join us if she is present. A period of silence followed (approx 2 minutes) before the EMF meter begins to flicker to Red.

11.23pm:

HM asks for confirmation of Peggys presence by asking her to once again affect the electromagnetic field in the room. The K2 meter once again flickers indicating a response. Temp noted at a steady 18 degrees. HM proceeds to question Peggy about her purpose for not crossing over into the light. She reports to the team that she sees a female standing by the altar, close to the doll. The woman is shaking her head as if saying no. HM asks what is wrong. At this point no other team members can see her however SH reports feeling suddenly colder.

11.27pm:

Temp reading 16 degrees. EMF no fluctuation.

11.30pm:

HM asks that Peggy help her by communicating her wishes through the pendulum and places her board on the table. The rest of the team close the circle. As she hold the pendulum there is a violent swing towards JH which makes several members jump. EMF fluctuation to orange. DG reports hearing very faint laughter but no others confirm this. Room temp 16 degrees.

11.32pm:

HM asks "was that you Peggy?" and there is a clear YES response via pendulum. HM proceeds through a series of questions, while confirming to the rest of the team that the figure is still present next to the altar.

Pendulum board divination (responses given in CAPITAL LETTERS):

"Do you fear crossing over into the light?" - N O F E A R

(pause - 3 seconds) N E X T

"Are you happy to be communicating with us?" - H A P P Y

(pause – 10 seconds) M O R E

"Peggy were you responsible for a recent health problem?" - NO

"Are you aware of the lady we mean? Katrin?" - YES

(long pause 55 seconds) W E A K

"What do you mean Peggy?" - T A K E C A R E H E A R T H E L P

"Were you trying to help?" - YES

"Do you feel you have a purpose here?" - YES (pause – 7 seconds) I KNOW

"What do you know Peggy?" - T O O M U C H F O R M E

At this point HM asked Peggy to step forward and make herself known to the group. MJ and JH both feel very cold. JH shows goosebumps on right arm. 11.55pm:

Temp reading 8 degrees.

JH comments that she can "see her". (a later description given by JH is vague but is confirmed by HM as a true likeness).

11.58pm:

MJ speaks out and asks Peggy to please respect his Church and to give the group clear indications of how to assist her.

There is a faint tapping sound on the window on the opposite side of the room to the altar. At this point HM tells the team that the apparition of Peggy has vanished. All members confirm hearing tapping.

12.00am:

HM requests that everyone remain holding hands, she attempts to reach Peggy once more. This time SH says someone's hand is on his shoulder. HM nods. He then comments "I can't feel it anymore". The sensation lasted for 5 seconds. HM addresses Peggy.

"Peggy we know you're still here so please speak with us".

There is a period of roughly 15 minutes in which apart from the odd creak from the building and sound of wind outside, nothing is recorded.

12.17am:

The pendulum moves and slowly directs itself to a series of letters.

The following is noted by DG:

L I N D Y H A R R Y G R E E N S T A R S O O N

MJ asks: "Can you be clearer Peggy?, Is this a warning?": YES

12.25am:

HM suggests JH speak directly to Peggy.

JH asks: "Peggy, do you need our help to move on?": NO

(pause – 12 seconds) T E L L T H E M JH replies: "Tell them what?": A L L 12.29am:

Temp reading 16 degrees.

12.30am:

HM asks "Peggy are you still here?" to which there is no reaction from the pendulum. The K2 meter is still on a green light and DG comments that the room feels 'normal again'. The team agree to close session. MJ blesses the group and the room and closes down the session aided by HM.

Session ends

The group session at the church was fascinating in that for the first time in this case, and only the 3rd time in my entire life, I saw a full apparition. A figure quite obviously a woman, but with no discernable facial features. Her face seemed almost blurred from my vision, and as quickly as she was there, she was gone, at least to my sight, but as she faded there seemed to be some little lights, very tiny twinkles a bit like to effect immediately before a migraine but smaller flashing dots. Very strange and something I'd never experienced before. Now I'm on the fence personally regarding these kinds of experiences, as we don't yet fully understand what causes visual phenomena of the type I experienced that night. Are these ghosts, for want of a better word, simply an imprint, replaying over time under the right conditions? To our knowledge there have been no other such sightings in

the church or surrounding area of an apparition and so the possibility that this experience came with someone, or something present in the room is increased. Whether residual or intelligent, and however it came to be, whether telepathic extraction or a genuine spirit in the room, for me this reinforced that we would have to continue investigating the doll.

Chapter 6
~ Dogs ~

"Please know that evil targets animals because animals are so sensitive. They make easy prey. Plus, targeting your pet is a way to hurt you. If the spirit takes away what you love, it can rip your life apart with ease. Dark spirits want to break you down, physically and emotionally. Just like some rotten people, evil spirits want to watch the world burn. When the spirits are finished with your animals, then they come for you". - Deborah Kauflin, Ph.D, author of 'Demon Attacks'

I have mentioned dogs several times already in this book, so let me explain in more detail my reason for considering experiences connected to dogs as an important feature in this case. The quote at the beginning of this chapter suggests that spirits affecting animals in a negative way are evil, however, I have my reservations about labeling Peggy as 'evil'.

On 26th February at 11:15am I received a message from Janice Carlton from Boise, Idaho which read:

"This is weird. Can dogs and cats sense evil? Since I opened the photo of that doll just my little terrier Molly has been snarling and growling at the screen. I'm a bit freaked".

This was the first in a string of such reports. Having not made this specific incident public, on 29th February at 10.35pm I received the following message from Darren Holder, a builder from Manchester in the UK.

"I've heard that animals are sensitive to spirits and ghosts and things, and never really believed it, but this is a bit strange. I saw a photo online of a doll you have, with blonde hair and a white dress. I was looking at it, not

really thinking much, when my staffie* Ronnie started barking at me. I've had him for 5 years and know him pretty well, and I could tell he was afraid. I stroked him and tried to calm him down but he was having none of it. He started spinning in circles, then he ran out of the bedroom and into the bathroom. When I followed him he was hiding in the bath! I've never seen him like it. He's not scared of anything. I didn't put 2 and 2 together until I carried him into the bedroom and he started barking again, this time at my PC. I closed the page with the dolls photo on, and he calmed down. Just thought you should know".

These 2 instances, in the space of a few days made me very curious. Both of these dogs appeared to be suddenly afraid. But what were they afraid of? Could they really sense something evil or threatening simply by seeing a photograph? Was a spirit connected to the doll actually present in there homes at those specific moments and was it that which the dogs were sensing? And if that was indeed the case, how was the spirit even aware when someone took an interest?

Again this could all come back to the idea that we all co-exist within a shared data bank made up of energy, and that possibly seeing the photograph of the doll, triggered something in these canines in a much more intense way, given their supposed predisposition to intuitive abilities, which led to them being able to subconsciously extract this negativity. The theme of the case was fast becoming one of more questions than answers as time went on.

*Staffie is a shortened version of Staffordshire Bull Terrier

Over the months that followed we received further reports of dogs behaving strangely around images or videos of Peggy, but it wasn't until April 2015 that things took a more serious turn, and is best explained in the words of Joan Cobb, a lady from Phoenix, Arizona who got in touch after a particularly sad incident.

```
Case: Peggy

Location: Phoenix, AZ

Date: 17th April 2015 - July  2015

In April I was watching a video of Peggy with
my dog next to me, and about 10-15 minutes
after I viewed it my dog suffered a seizure.
She had never had a seizure in her whole life.
I took her to the vet and he couldn't find any
reason for her to have had a seizure. The vet
checked her out completely, he ran CT scans and
MRI's on her and couldn't find anything that
would cause her to have a  seizure.

She came home and was completely normal again.
No lingering signs of her seizures, until I
watched the video again, and almost immediately
she had another seizure. That's what finally
flipped the switch for me that it had to be
Peggy. Twice I watched the video, and twice she
had a seizure right after. She has since passed
away and I feel the connection between Peggy,
other dogs behaving oddly, and what happened to
my baby to be too strong to be  coincidence.

Joan Cobb Phoenix, AZ
```

We continue to find it difficult to explain what happened to Joans beloved dog, and others like her. Many of us believe that animals have a strong sixth sense when it comes to ghosts and the spirit world generally, even believing that animals can sense danger or evil, but wouldn't we then be getting reports of cats also acting oddly? Well apparently not. Despite being commonly thought of as witches familiars, creatures of mystery and so on, there are many theorists who believe that it is dogs who have a very high level of ESP (Extra sensory perception) and in an article by Stanley Coren, Professor of Psychology at the University of British Columbia, entitled 'Clairvoyant Canines' he explores this theory.

"The belief that dogs have psychic abilities runs deeply through many cultures. Some believe that Dogs can see devils, angels and ghosts. Probably the most common example of a dog anticipating an event occurring is the familiar observation that dogs seem to know exactly when their owners are coming home".

Dr Rupert Sheldrake, who holds a Ph.D. in biochemistry, argues that *"the most convincing evidence for telepathy between people and animals comes from the study of dogs that know when their owners are coming home".*

The most closely studied case of supposed canine ESP involves a mixed-breed terrier named Jaytee, who lived in Ramsbottom, England with his owner Pamela Smart. Jaytee seemed to anticipate Pam's return by running to the window, or outside to sit on the porch, just about the time that his mistress was beginning her return trip home. This anticipation occurred even when Pam's schedule was irregular and her travel times were unknown by other members of her family. In an attempt to verify Jaytee's telepathic abilities, the Austrian State Television network sent two film crews. One crew followed Pam as she walked around the town, and the other stayed at home and continuously filmed Jaytee. After a couple of hours, Pam and her crew decided to head home, and at that very moment Jaytee went out on the porch and remained there until

Pam returned. The results of this experiment received a lot of media attention, with television commentators describing the dog as "psychic" and "always correct in his anticipations."

Sheldrake decided to invite a team of researchers, headed by psychologist Richard Wiseman of the University of Hertfordshire, to test Jaytee's telepathy. The results of this research have been published in the *British Journal of Psychology*. Wiseman's first task was to eliminate any possible non-telepathic cues that might trigger the dog's behaviour. This meant that Pam could not leave and return at regular times, or use a familiar car. They also had to eliminate any possible cues the dog might pick up from the behaviours of other people in the house. To do this, Wiseman and his team designed an experiment in which no one, including Pam, would know in advance exactly when she would start her journey home. Specifically, they took Pam to a remote location and used a special calculator to generate a random time for her return. Pam was only told that they were going to return home a few seconds before the group actually started back.

Jaytee predicted her return accurately each time.

Of course this is just one case. But there are countless like it out there. Dr Rupert Sheldrake published an article in The Daily Mail in 2012 in which he explains that the Western world is ignoring the ability of dogs to anticipate disasters and potentially connect to the spirit world.

"Some animals seem to sense when their owners have had accidents or have died in distant places — as documented on my database of more than 5,000 case histories involving psychic phenomena in animals. This includes 177 cases of dogs apparently responding to the death or

suffering of their absent masters or mistresses, mostly by howling, whining or whimpering before any of the family or friends are aware it has happened". - Dr R Sheldrake.

So if science is taking this seriously, we should too. I am inclined to believe that the dogs we have heard about in relation to Peggys case, have been demonstrating a high level of ESP, an ability that's quite beyond most humans. What is unclear, and admittedly alarming, is just what their ESP was picking up on. All of the dogs we've heard about have reacted in a negative and fearful way to images or videos of Peggy.

Some believe that Peggy, or possibly another spirit connected to Peggy or the doll, means harm to these pets. Others are more inclined to believe that rather than an entity meaning direct harm to an animal, it is more likely that the dogs are picking up on something they find naturally terrifying, and it is this fact that is causing them to behave in the way they do, and in extreme cases to suffer health problems, rather than the entity or spirit actually intending harm directly.

We continue to receive reports. Some examples follow:

```
Witness Testimony Case: Peggy

Location: Mounds View, Minnesota Date: April
2015

I got the idea to ask Peggy to visit me in my
dream one night right before I fell asleep, and
I think she did. In my dream, Kyle (my
boyfriend) and I sat down at the dining room
table and he was asking me if there's a demon,
how do you get it to go away. I started telling
him to start by saying I plead the blood of
Jesus Christ over myself and this home, then I
looked out the window to see a weird, female,
marsh looking, demented demon creature (more
```

human form though) in my neighbors yard which was right across from our windows. I pointed it out to him saying do you see that demon? Right then it appeared right next to one of the windows. And Kyles like "oh, geez, yeah." Then I decided to try making it go away.

You know how in dreams when you try to run, it feels like you're running through water? Like you can't really run?

Well that's how I felt trying to talk and cast or away, I felt frightened and my chest got tight.

When I was trying to do that she kept saying some scary foreign language to me to try to counter what I was saying. She was scary, and then I woke up in a snap and my heart was beating so fast and I got so scared.

I woke up a bit before 3:09am, and I stayed awake that whole time until 4:20am. At that point Kyle came into my bedroom, and there was something really wrong with Maizey, his dog. We ended up having to take her in to the Emergency vet right away to get her looked at. She had some severe GI thing and they said it's good we got her in when we did as she would have died that night. I can't help thinking it's connected to Peggy and my dream, although why would she harm a dog?

Tiffany Bovitz Minnesota

Witness Testimony Case: Peggy

Location: Norwich, UK Date: June 2015

I breed Labradors, and honestly I have never had much interest in the paranormal, but when my 18 year old daughter started taking an interest I thought I'd check out what she was viewing online, being a protective Mum. As a dog breeder I have kennels in the rear garden where we keep the adults, and most of the time the pups too, except of course when they're newborn. About 3 weeks ago our oldest female

Holly gave birth to a litter of stillborn pups. We were devastated. Her pregnancy had been fine and she had been checked by the vet only 2 weeks prior to delivery. All was well. Now obviously I can't prove it, but after reading about this doll of yours and what it apparently has done to other dogs, I can't get it out of my head that it is somehow connected. We've never had a tragedy of this level. Occasionally you might get 1 stillborn, but 99% of the time we have healthy happy puppies. My daughter had seen a video of the doll about a month ago, then started showing me a few other photos, often around Hollys feeding time as that's when we were all in the kitchen together. So Holly was always around when we had the photos up on screen. I know on one occasion she was whining a lot but at the time we thought it was just normal pains, now I just don't know.

Julie Watson Norwich

Witness Testimony Case: Peggy

Location: Solihull, UK Date: August 2015

As mad as it sounds now, I used to have a picture of Peggy as my screensaver on my phone. My 5 year old corgi Peanut had never taken any notice of my phone before, but as soon as I changed my screensaver to a picture of Peggys face he seemed to hate it! He'd bark whenever the screen lit up with a message or call, or run into another room. I even found it half buried in the garden (where he does his business!) once after searching all over the house for it. He just didn't like that photo. I can't think of any other reason for it, especially as since I changed the screensaver to a photo of my son he's now fine with my phone again. Really weird.

Brian Cartwright Solihull near Birmingham

It has been suggested that we take Peggy along to a dog shelter to monitor the reactions of various dogs,

however given the quite serious nature of some of the events that have happened, we feel it a potential risk and at this stage have ruled out 'experimenting' in this way. Quite rightly friends of ours who have dogs will now no longer bring them to our home as even the most committed paranormal skeptics, would rather not take the risk when it comes to their canine companions it seems. Just incase.

Chapter 7
~ Considerations ~

In May 2015, not least as a result of the continued reports of illness and disturbing experiences made by members of the public, we decided that it may be in the public interest, at least until we had a better idea of what we were dealing with, to withdraw details of our ongoing investigation from our main social media pages and website. Before making the decision final, we asked the online community for their thoughts. The case up to this point had, after all, been strongly led by the experiences of the public. There was a strong desire by many people to continue to know how things were unfolding, and so it was suggested that a dedicated group be formed, giving those who wished to keep up to date the option to do so, while protecting those who felt they were being affected by her images and videos. It was a wonderful idea and gave us the peace of mind, at least to some extent, of knowing that anyone who happened to find an image of Peggy in their newsfeed had given their consent to do so.

The group was formed, and as promised no further images, videos or updates relating to Peggy were posted on our main pages. It was intriguing to us how many people, despite being previously affected by Peggy, chose to join the group and continue to engage in discussions about her. For most I assume it was a way of trying to come to terms with their experiences. Maybe interacting with others who had experienced unexplainable phenomena was a way of validating things.

A strong sense of community quickly formed and the support group members were showing for each other was evident.

Suddenly more people than ever were opening up about things that had happened to them, knowing they were in a non judgmental environment and could do so knowing that not only would we read their comments and respond, but that they may also find answers or comfort from sharing with like minded people.

We are very aware of our responsibilities in terms of what we put out there, and quite rightly. To anyone who genuinely has a passion and respect for the unknown, that is the deal. When you're working in the field of the paranormal you can't make light of the possible repercussions. If you're daily routine involves attempting communication with the spirit world, and subsequently sharing your experiences with the world, then you must be careful. We are keen to ensure that no-one dabbles in the kind of work we do. You can't enter into serious paranormal investigation half heartedly, or as a bit of fun, although of course we do enjoy what we do and have been known to enjoy a giggle at our own expense, especially at 3am in the morning when we're sitting around a table wanting to speak to the dead! However to think that forming a connection to those in the afterlife is purely for entertainment is the kind of attitude that can lead people down a reckless path of improper Ouija board use, tarot cards and invocation rituals. I personally believe that if there are such things as spirits, then they are likely to be around us all of the time. They can't always see us, and possibly are going about their day to day existence blissfully unaware of us, unaware they are dead even in some cases! But every now and then the veil lifts and we catch a glimpse of each other. In many ways, these kinds of spirits, some call them "in limbo", must be just as afraid as we are.

To them we may well be the apparition! It all comes down to our own individual perception of reality. We have ours, and I'm sure those in spirit have theirs.

I don't believe for a second that everyone who passes over from this life is suddenly gifted with an all seeing all knowing ability, or an overwhelming sense of calm. I think that for many of us, passing over will happen so suddenly that our minds and souls will take a little more time than our bodies to leave this earthly realm. If you turn off a light bulb, the electricity itself still exists. The bulb is simply not making use of it anymore.

In truth I don't think we will ever fully understand the different layers of existence, not until the time comes for each of us to pass from one to the next, and maybe not even then as there could well be another 3, 4, 5, 100 layers to come after that for each of us. Maybe it's some kind of unwritten law of the universe, maybe it simply comes down to physics why most of us can only speculate, and catch the odd hint at what is to come once we have no further use of our earthly vessels.

Maybe most of us simply do not have access to the part of the brain, which can receive and decode images and messages from spirit (the part which may be more active in children but in most of us – those who later consider themselves psychic mediums excluded – becomes closed down through learned rationalization of experiences as we age). Interestingly, there seems to be some strength in the idea that as we age, and specifically as we begin to reach the end of our earthly lives, this part of the brain begins to, for want of a better word, reactivate.

Staff working in care homes or hospitals have often reported that residents or patients will comment that they have seen their loved ones in dreams, or have known they will be coming for them soon shortly before they pass away. Are we all part of a cycle? Both newborn babies and the elderly could technically be seen as closer to another layer or dimension than someone in middle age if this were the case. Or is it more likely that those in the spirit world are subtly aware of when a loved ones time in their physical body is due to cease, and so have access to them in a way they didn't throughout their lives?

Questions upon questions once more. But back to the point...Peggy.

I had decided in early April to put questions, sent from followers, directly to Peggy and to film it to see what happened. I had my EMF meter to hand too. Hazel suggested that I use the basement and set the scene properly as that would hopefully help with results. I sat there with Peggy in front of me, candles lit and peoples questions in my hand. I felt odd but knew it was good to let some of our followers have their questions and concerns voiced directly in the presence of the doll. It wasn't the most exciting of sessions however I did get EMF responses to some of the points and they seemed appropriately timed. What was strange was that throughout the session I hadn't noticed the doll moving at all. Not until she fell and knocked the camera over. When reviewing the footage I sped it up by 3 times it's original speed, and it then was obvious that she was leaning more and more away from me with each second that passed. The clip was shared on our YouTube channel but I couldn't have predicted that it would be picked up by the local and national news and so I was totally unprepared for what followed. Paranormal websites such as 'Unexplained Mysteries' were suddenly posting threads discussing Peggy and my work and there were even some personal comments about me which of course are inevitable. I admit that I hadn't made an effort with my appearance on the day that the footage was taken as wasn't leaving the house however to be likened to an escaped mental patient, or an ageing hippy was kind of hurtful I must confess!

Something that worried us more than the immature comments of a few individuals online however was how our immediate friends, family and neighbours would feel now that what we were dealing with was out in the open for all to see. Not everyone would feel comfortable knowing they were living next door to a couple who investigated the paranormal and owned a haunted doll!

I lost sleep imagining lynch mobs outside the house and looks of disapproval at the school gates. On the contrary however we have been amazed by the positive response, in particular from family who far from disowning us or calling us crazy, have embraced what we do and most of them are equally as intrigued as we are – although most of them choose not to meet Peggy for themselves.

A couple of months after the video of Peggy and I in our basement was shown on the Daily Mail website my sister in law was watching it at home and suddenly felt unwell. She decided to lie down and a piercing headache followed. She had to rest for about an hour before feeling herself again. She messaged me later that day as was quite surprised by the reaction to Peggy, given that she's not at all impressionable or suggestible! It was unexpected. A few weeks later she had been showing the same clip to a friend of hers, but didn't explain anything about Peggy, other than the fact she herself had suffered a sudden headache after watching it first time around. After they'd finished watching it the friend laughed "well I don't have a headache, but has anyone ever had chest pains!?".

She was experiencing sudden chest pain that went once she stopped watching Peggy. It's personal accounts like this, from people I love and trust that add to my curiosity. The power of suggestion is always in the back of my mind when hearing experiences, but I know my sister in law, and I know that she is not easily manipulated into thinking or feeling anything. Her friend, well she had never heard of anyone having chest pains before, and it was the first time she had seen the clip. The incidents seemed to leave them a little freaked out to say the least.

For us the most important consideration has always been the safety of our home and our children. When you investigate the paranormal, you understand that there is an element of uncertainty, both with regards to what you may experience and also in how those experiences will manifest, both emotionally and physically. What people don't always necessarily understand is that in owning a haunted object, you are in effect welcoming a haunting, or encouraging a haunting within your home. A scary prospect for some people, but given that the idea of ghosts and spirits being real has been something that has followed me for most if not my entire life, I can honestly say that until having children, small innocent and vulnerable little people, I never considered the dangers or repercussions. Before becoming a mother my curiosity and intrigue for the unknown superseded my fear.

Suddenly when you become a parent you view the world in general quite differently, or at least I did. You sometimes cannot see past the potential danger in something, and often to the detriment of your childs enjoyment. Playing on a climbing frame for example used to be a fun idea when you were younger, but now your own offspring are scaling the metal bars to the top all you can imagine is that they could fall and hurt themselves. You notice that the bars are wet, that their shoes don't have good grips, that their jacket has loops that could get caught and other small, but potentially key factors. It's like we arereconditioned or reconfigured with this 'Danger Identification Programme' that we cannot switch off. I suppose it's simply a case of ensuring survival. If we were living in caves thousands of years ago we would be constantly on the look out for predators and ways to source food for our young to keep them alive and well. The time period changes but the inbuilt instinct remains, for most of us at least. When you welcome potential paranormal happenings into your home, it brings with it the added burden of worry and guilt, should anything happen. For a while I struggled to deal with this and when my first daughter was very young, around 8 months old, we had a frightening experience, which made me reconsider my pursuit of supernatural experiences. I should make it clear that this was well before Peggy entered our lives. It had been an ordinary day and I was feeding my daughter at around 6pm. Suddenly I heard the sound of the backdoor handle turning as if someone was trying to get in. This would be worrying in itself, however what made this more disturbing was the fact that we had recently added a conservatory to the rear of our home, and so what had been the backdoor, was now an internal door leading to the conservatory. Now my first thought was "someone's in the conservatory!" I picked up my daughter, turned off all of the lights and waited. Again I heard the door handle, and as I peered out into the kitchen I saw the old black iron handle move down slightly, and knew that someone, or something was putting pressure on the other side of handle. I quickly darted back into the living room and closed the door. While sitting on the sofa, holding my daughter and furiously trying to call my Husband I noticed strange patterns of light on the carpet. As I looked up I realized they was being caused by the chandelier, swinging above our heads. It lasted no more than 10 seconds but seemed to go on forever.

Suddenly all was calm and still once more. Thankfully my daughter was too young to know anything was going on. That experience stayed with me, and was one of many experiences in that house. We moved shortly after, but not due to the experiences more for practical reasons.

And so I was faced with the reality of paranormal activity occurring under the same roof as my children. I'm sure many of you reading this feel that under no circumstances would you allow this to happen, but bear in mind that this has been my career for 17 years, and while my children are my priority, I cannot change who I am. My children have never been harmed, or felt afraid in our home as noticeable instances are rare even today, and we make sure that any channel of communication that is opened by us is properly closed. We never use Ouija boards and never conduct séances at home either. I believe strongly that your home should be your sanctuary and completely separate from work.

The only area we use for the purposes of our research is our basement –

where our children never go, and have no interest in going.

Of course when they're older they may decide they are uncomfortable with their parents being involved in the unpredictable world of the paranormal. If so, we will give it all up in a heartbeat. Nothing means more to us than their happiness.

Chapter 8
~ Derby Gaol ~

We had been asked many times whether we would be taking Peggy to any events or making her available for the public to meet but in all honesty I resisted the idea simply because I didn't feel it was appropriate to do so for a long time. Apart from anything else, given the serious reactions people had been having from just her photograph I wasn't too comfortable with a crowd of people being face to face with her for fear of what may happen – I don't think any kind of insurance policy covers that!

It took months of contemplation before I finally decided that in the name of research, and with the help of willing and informed adults, we would conduct a group experiment with her in the form of an evening at a haunted location. Why a haunted location? There are those, myself included, who believe that by introducing an object that has a link to the spirit world, into an environment where ghosts and spirits are already present, we can strengthen that connection and open a clearer and more obvious doorway or portal. In other words, we felt that maybe Peggy could act as some form of conductor or maybe even become some form of trigger object by spiking the curiosity of any spirits present. So that was it, decision made. I knew I didn't want to profit from the event, as it would be very much a trial and error evening where people would be potentially putting themselves at risk by being in close proximity to Peggy, and so chose CLIC Sargent Childrens Cancer charity as our recipient for funds raised. For us we would be gaining something far more significant than money in exchange for offering this opportunity to meet Peggy. We would hopefully gain some form of proof, or evidence that this spirit or spirits could affect the living physically.

We would have our guinea pigs!

The next part of the process would be choosing the venue. This was relatively easy. For many years I have admired the work of Richard Felix. His vast historical knowledge and theatrical delivery of gruesome tales and chilling ghost stories made him the perfect choice for TV's Most Haunted and he was fantastic in his role as Paranormal Historian, but personally it has always been his own work that I've found more interesting, especially his "Ghost Tour of Great Britain" DVD's of which "Ghosts of Chillingham Castle" is a particular favourite. What I admire about Richard is that he doesn't fall foul of amateur dramatics when in a haunted location. You won't find a great deal of staggered night vision footage or EMF meters in Richards DVD's, and he freely admits that he is terrified of ghosts, but fascinated by them. He places emphasis on the history of locations and hearing individual accounts from people who have experienced something paranormal. My interest meant that I had long held a desire to visit Derby Gaol, owned and operated by Richard. A few emails later and it was all arranged. We would be holding our charity event at Derby Gaol on October 23rd 2015. I was excited and nervous, and was keeping my fingers crossed that no-one would be hurt or negatively affected.

I knew the idea wouldn't be something Hazel would want to be involved in, not because she would disagree with us experimenting in this way, but more that she would feel incredibly uncomfortable being in the limelight herself, and I respect that. In fact it adds weight to my admiration of her. I did feel though that it would be very important to have the assistance of someone psychically gifted, but knowing who to trust might be difficult. The world is awash with people who claim to be able to communicate with the spirit world, and working in paranormal investigation we are regularly approached by people looking to offer us their services. I am not overly cynical, but I am cautious.

Fate was to intervene and around the time we secured our booking at Derby Gaol, I began chatting to Ian Griffiths on Facebook after we had been commenting on the same post in a paranormal group. Ian is a Psychic Medium with plenty of experience and we spoke about various aspects of the paranormal. Ian has a great reputation amongst those who have experienced his gift and it didn't take long for me to see he was the real deal. Ian explained that he had been taking a break from his mediumship but had decided that now was a good time to make a return. He was curious about our work and haunted objects generally and we chatted about some of our individual experiences and I warmed to him immediately.

I spoke to Simon and he agreed that we should ask Ian if he might help out at the event. Conveniently enough it turned out that Ian lives a short drive from Derby Gaol and had already met Richard on several paranormal investigations in and around Derby and Burton-on-Trent. Fate indeed. Ian was up for the idea and meeting Peggy. He mentioned that he always worked with a paranormal investigator called Paul Bosworth and asked if he could also come along. I said of course, the more the merrier. The event was advertised and tickets started selling. This added to both my excitement and also my anxiety regarding everyones safety. In these situations Simon is always the voice of reason and kept reminding me that everyone who wanted to come along was coming with their eyes open, fully aware of the experiences that other people attributed to Peggy.

As we sold more tickets, and I chatted to those who were coming along on the night, I discovered that each of them had their own sometimes very personal reasons for wanting to meet her. Far from being terrified, many of the people who were coming along to the event felt very warm and loving towards Peggy, in a parental, quite protective way, which was quite unexpected.

As the months passed we began making plans and under the guidance of Hazel we prepared Peggy. We knew that there would always be an element of uncertainty when it came to placing Peggy in a new environment, however Hazel had given us some protection, individually and around Peggy

(Hazel still felt that there was another spirit, a darker entity present around the doll and she was keen to do all she could to keep it's influence limited if possible). The plan was that the staff of Derby Gaol would organize and deliver a series of paranormal activities for guests. In hindsight we should have taken care of this element of the evening ourselves as in all honesty the event itself didn't progress as we'd expected and we didn't have time for many things including the human pendulum. But back to Peggy...

When we arrived in Derby with Peggy on Friday 23rd October it was roughly 7pm and we made our way to our hotel The Jurys Inn, just a stones throw from Derby Gaol. While we didn't discuss it at the time, both Simon and I have since spoken about the feeling of there being 3 of us throughout our stay.

We felt watched the entire time we were in our room, and neither of us slept at all following the event. Whether this was purely psychological, or something more spiritual of course we can't possibly know, but it's interesting how Peggy, or at least the doll, is in our home 24 hours a day 7 days a week and we very rarely feel a tangible presence and not often in the way we felt it then. Our guests for the evening were due to arrive at 8pm and so after dumping our bags and freshening up we headed straight back out into the night. I must admit it was a very surreal experience, walking through a strange city (neither of us had never been to Derby prior to the event) with Peggy in her large black holdall, neither Simon nor I fully knowing what to expect from the hours that would follow. We arrived to find Edd Felix (Richards son) building a fire in the day room, a surprisingly cosy and inviting room considering the original purpose of the building itself! Warm red brickwork, sloping floors and exposed beams provided a historical meeting place with the unusual gothic hand shaped candle holders on each table adding a suitably macabre and sinister feel. In one corner of the room, perched high above the fire was a CCTV monitor showing the inside of the condemned cell. This would be Peggys home for the remainder of the evening with the night vision providing everyone with a great view of any activity that may occur.

Ian and Paul set up talking boards (different to Ouija boards as they are self made and self designed and omit certain elements found on a traditional Ouija, these "talk boards" as they are often referred to amongst investigators work incredibly well). We placed Peggy in her position in the condemned cell and left her for a few moments. I'd been advised by Hazel to allow some time prior to allowing people to attempt communication with her. It wasn't long before we realized that things were going to get quite interesting.

Myself, Simon, Ian and Paul were in the cell next to Peggys and I was crouched down arranging trigger objects on the bed (less a bed more a plank of wood in actual fact!). Paul and Ian were attempting to contact the spirit world using the board and Paul asked for a sign if someone was present with us in the room.

I suddenly felt someone push my back as if trying to make me lose my balance.

"I felt that!" I said with surprise. After a few more minutes in the room Ian walked next door into Peggys cell. We gradually followed one by one and as soon as we were all in the cell together Simon and I both commented that we could smell flowers, roses. I was certain it was roses. Almost as suddenly as it arrived, the smell vanished. We checked for air fresheners and other possible explanations but it left us quite dumbfounded. There is a belief amongst some paranormal circles that the Holy Spirit brings with it the smell of roses, while others believe simply that the smell indicates spirit presence. I obviously cannot say with any certainty either way, however I have never experienced such a sudden and obvious fragrance as I did that night, especially given that it was gone within seconds. I remain intrigued by that.

As guests began arriving we took some time to chat to everyone. It provided us with a rare opportunity to socialize with people we usually only get chance to communicate with via social media, which was a real treat. Once everyone was seated we ran through some introductions followed by a talk by Edd on the history and ghost stories of the gaol itself. We then gave guests the opportunity to enter either of the cells to have a go at communicating using the boards. Of course everyone started queuing for Peggys cell and we were struck by the excitement that was all around us. The chance to see Peggy up close and personal was truly a thrilling prospect for many who were armed with cameras and EMF meters. The first 6 or 7 people managed to sit down around the board and the session began, with eager onlookers struggling to see past each other and down onto the board. I wasn't present at this stage as was busy arranging equipment elsewhere and checking the register to make sure everyone had signed in.

About 10 minutes had passed and I looked up to see Simon walking towards me. I knew he wanted to tell me something but I couldn't be sure if it was good or bad. I braced myself. "Whats happening?" I asked.

"I think she's here" he said.

"what do you mean? Peggy?" I asked with a nod, almost certain that was who he meant.

"Yep. The glass, it started moving and spelt out Peggy". Simon looked quite surprised and given that it was so early on in the evening I must confess that I too was slightly stunned. However, this was why we were here and if I'd had any doubt about whether or not Peggy (or any spirit present with the doll) wanted an audience, that doubt was now gone. It was crystal clear that this was a spirit who wanted to be recognized and addressed by the living. Simon began making his way back up to the cell and I followed, video camera at the ready. As I got near the cell one of the guests, Letitia Hemmings was trying to get out of there.

"Are you ok?" I asked. Letitia pulled me to one side and began telling me that she had felt incredibly uncomfortable while sitting around the board, and had only just gone back into the cell after having to leave once already. She felt that Peggy, or another presence didn't want her in there.

What follows is Letitia's statement relating to her experience.

Witness Testimony

Case: Peggy

Location: Derby Gaol Event 2015 Date: October 2015

Meeting Peggy was an amazing experience. I was a little nervous at first but I was totally drawn to her. In the condemned cell I sat across the room from her. When Ouija board sessions started I sat down the furthest away from Peggy, she said a few things on the board in answer to people questions. When I spoke Peggy told me to leave which I did without hesitation. When I went back I actually got to sit next to Peggy. As I was sitting there I got a awful burning sensation in-between my legs which was so bad I actually left the room, I was quiet worried to go to the bathroom as I imagined there to be a lot of blood. When I had calmed down I went back into the condemned cell with Peggy and carried on the investigation. While I was sitting there I had a vision of a woman being raped and I saw a lot of blood. Not long after that vision I had butterflies in my tummy. I asked Peggy a few times if I could touch her and her answer through the board was "no", then "get out".

It was like 2 different spirits.

Letitia Hemmings

Ghostly Echoes Paranormal Birmingham, UK

This was obviously distressing for her, and for me also as I felt that in some way I knew, or at least was familiar to some degree with the activity and energy that accompanied Peggy. What Letitia had experienced seemed purposefully targeted and malicious, designed to make her feel pain and discomfort. I had heard of many cases whereby a spirit will transfer feelings, either physical or emotional, onto the living as a way of trying to show maybe how they died, and this seemed to be the way Letitia had taken it too. If it was in some way caused as a result of the ongoing communication session with Peggy then I was now even more wary than before.

I joined the group in the cell and watched as question after question was posed to the invisible force in the room. EMF meters spiked immediately after questions in a way that seemed far too accurate to be random fluctuations and it seemed to everyone present that a doorway to the spirit world was undeniably open. We were later informed that during the board session with Peggy, those guests who had remained in the day room watching the CCTV had all seen a shadow, which appeared to move slightly to the left of the doll where no-one had been standing. We checked and the light source outside of the room did not cause normal shadows to be cast in this way what's more, once the session was over, and EMF meters ceased registering changes in the electromagnetic field, the shadow was no longer visible. Had this been Peggy, or possibly another spirit?

I took a series of photographs into the cell after the session, one of which appeared to show a shadow.

If this is a spirit it appears to be male, at least to my eyes.

Following the initial activity and communication from Peggy the evening progressed at a less intense pace with a fascinating talk from Richard Felix following by our charity raffle prize draw. At just after 2.30am, tired but wired, we began saying our goodbyes to everyone, feeling certain that most of our paths would cross again at some point in the future.

The next day we felt relieved that the event had not only been a success in terms of raising money for CLIC Sargent, but that we'd had no serious incidents, although Letitias experience still concerned me. If taking Peggy to Derby gaol had shown me anything, it was that things were only just beginning.

with Richard Felix at Derby Gaol, September 2015

Chapter 9
~ Peggy meets Zak ~

I'd received an email in late April 2015 from Aaron Bengston, a producer from New York, who wanted to have a chat with me about potentially appearing on a new TV show he was working on, although his email was very brief and no details were given. I replied and we arranged a time to chat over the phone. A few days later and a conference call came through with Aaron and the Producer Casey Dale. As Casey was explaining their idea for a new show he casually asked "Have you heard of Ghost Adventures?". I laughed and replied

"I think most people have heard of Ghost Adventures!".

He went on to explain that Zak Bagans had seen Peggys story on the Daily Mail website and was intrigued by the sheer volume of people that were being affected by her. What's more, he wanted to meet me and discuss the case and was extending an invitation to fly us over to Las Vegas, with Peggy, to take part in a new show.

My initial reaction wasn't as you might expect. Far from being excited I felt worried. "Isn't Zak terrified of dolls?" I queried.

Casey laughed.

"Well, yeah he is. He likes to face his fears though, to get scared".

"Right, ok, erm…great!" was all I could think of to say.

We chatted for a while and I ran through some of the experiences people had been having and explained all about Katrin Reedik and her heart attack. Casey thought it would be a good idea to invite Katrin on the show too to discuss what happened, and I agreed. I had never met Katrin in person and after what had happened, I thought it would be good for us all. Casey explained that as this was a new show we had to keep it entirely under wraps, which meant making no reference to the production on social media or to anyone not involved. I guess you'd say it was on a strictly 'need to know' basis. Zak was yet to announce his plans and with the industry being as competitive as it is they were desperate to prevent details being leaked. It was agreed that I would be contacted again as soon as they had scheduled in their filming dates. I explained that as I had 2 small children I was keen to not be away from home for too long. Casey understood, and given that filming was due to commence in December 2015 I made it clear that providing I wouldn't be expected to miss my daughters first nativity play, then I would do it. It may sound crazy to some of you reading this, that I would potentially pass up on the opportunity to be flown to Las Vegas, meet Zak and take part in his new show, all for a pre-school nativity (that actually only lasted 20 minutes and in which my daughter didn't have a main role) but as a mother these are the occasions that you simply don't get back. I would have forever regretted missing that, and nothing could be worth a lifetime of regret in regards to my children.

Thankfully I got the call to say that filming would begin on December 7th, a week before the nativity play, and that I'd be needed for 4 days. I breathed a huge sigh of relief and began making plans. It was agreed that Simon would accompany me, but even so, I still felt uncomfortable at the idea of taking Peggy on a packed plane with hundreds of other people, for 10 hours. I have no fear of flying, maybe just the natural fleeting worry as the plane takes off, but the thought of having her with us seemed to me to be tempting fate, or pushing our luck just a little too much, and if there is one place you do not want to be pushing your luck it's at 35,000 feet! I was also aware of how awkward it could be at the check in gate to be accompanied by a 3ft plastic doll who would have very likely have needed her own seat due to size alone! I decided I would ship her over in advance.

Jami Schultz, the production manager had been in contact with me for several weeks over email and had arranged our flights and hotel and made the concierge aware that a 'special' package would be arriving from the UK. We would not explain exactly what that package contained however on the customs label! Not that they would have believed us anyway. Jami was great throughout the entire process. No question was too small to ask and she was, and continues to be to this day, incredibly helpful and supportive.

I think there were a lot of nerves on behalf of both parties, us and the production team, with regards to Peggys safety, and I was asked to sign an insurance document incase she got lost. Admittedly the thought had crossed my mind, and I was more than happy to do whatever I needed to incase the worst happened although the thought of losing her forever was sickening.

As December approached I began dreading leaving my children. I had never been away from them for more than 1 night and with the time difference it would mean we would be away from them for 5 nights and I genuinely did not know how I would cope with that. I know there are parents who have to leave their children for much longer periods as a result of their profession, and I suppose it can become an occupational hazard for many, but for me, it's not something that I am accustomed to or if I'm honest, not something I want to be accustomed to. I told myself that it would fly as we would be busy, and with the girls being at their grandparents for the duration, we knew they were in safe hands. But still I felt like I had a rock in my stomach. I knew I wouldn't want to Skype back home as seeing their little faces and not being able to kiss them would have made things worse, and possibly have upset them too and so on the morning of December 5th Simon and I stood and waved off our girls as they drove away with my parents, and I cried. A small part of me felt that I shouldn't be leaving them, especially with our youngest Connie only being 18 months old. But it was done, and now we had to focus.

We arrived at Heathrow airport 2 hour early and in an attempt to kill time, we pulled up a stool at the nearest bar. We knew Peggy had arrived safely at Palms Place Hotel as I'd received an email from the front desk with details of where to collect my "package" from. Before we knew it we were boarding and settling in for the 10-hour flight. Simon is not a good flyer in fact as each year passes he becomes worse and so this was going to be testing for him. The longest flight we'd had prior to Vegas was from London to Canada, which took just under 9 hours and we remembered only too well how painful (in more ways than 1!) that had been. This time though, with larger seats, more space to move around and the added luxury of a free bar, we started choosing which movie to watch first. The flight went relatively smoothly, although sleep escaped both of us unfortunately, and we landed in Vegas at the best time you could possibly land in Vegas…nighttime. The lights looked fantastic from the air and the excitement and adrenalin kicked in. We had spotted Katrin as we boarded the plane but were yet to speak to her. As we all made our way outside the airport and towards the waiting production car, we began chatting, albeit wearily. Just a short 10-minute drive and we pulled up outside Palms Place Hotel. For those of you who have never been to Las Vegas I'll explain something. Every hotel is also a casino. Well maybe not every hotel, but a good 99% of them. They are mini resorts and you can get whatever your heart desires any time of day or night. It sounds amazing, but when you wake in the morning and go down for breakfast, there is something highly unnerving about seeing the same people sitting at the same slot machines they had been keeping company when you walked past them the previous evening.

Had they been home in between? Unlikely. Casinos offer you everything you need, and a lot that you don't! You can eat your 3 meals a day and drink copious amounts of any beverage imaginable without even having to stand up. Once seated at a machine a waitress heads straight over to you to take your order, and those scantily clad waitresses keep it coming. Not an ideal vision at 7am.

Given that our body clocks were all over the place, Simon and I had little more than 2 hours sleep in that first 24 hours. We had the day to ourselves on Sunday and so took the opportunity to see the sights. We had a wonderful day visiting the various casinos and bars, taking in the breathtaking

Bellagio fountains musical display and of course, one of our favourite mutual pastimes, people watching. You see it all in Las Vegas, Elvis chatting to Marilyn Monroe over a Big Mac, being a particular highlight for me.

After walking until we physically could walk no more we returned to our hotel room exhausted but with a packed day of memories. The days that followed would be about to give us a whole load more too.

At 10am on Monday 7th December the production car picked

us up and drove us to the filming location, in downtown Las Vegas. As is usually the case with a brand new TV show, the set was inconspicuous. Just a fairly regular looking building in a regular looking street, however the presence of Zaks Bentley Continental and Aarons huge pick up truck outside did trigger a few glances from passers by. But on the whole, a very discreet set up. We were greeted by Jami and Casey and is was good to put faces to the people I'd been in contact with for over 6 months. Both were excited to catch a glimpse of Peggy, and looked concerned to see me step out of the car without her. "Don't worry" I said smiling. "She's in the back".

Casey had an old suitcase ready as a prop to put her into, but had underestimated her size and so he asked if we could go to plan B. Placing a black bag over her head. This was something I hadn't expected and Casey explained that it was at Zaks request, and when we met with Zak I understood why. He was in 2 minds about actually seeing Peggy himself as had been thinking about what had happened to other people. Also being a dog lover, Zak was concerned by the reports of seizures and fatalities. We decided to go with the flow and as and when Zak was ready to remove the bag then it would happen. After some time relaxing over Starbucks coffee and beef jerky (that kept Si happy!) things began moving. We were mic'd up and made to look presentable. When the door opened into the museum set it was like stepping into a creepy gothic haunted house. While we'd been chatting it was explained to us that it only took the team a few weeks to get the set looking just right, which is amazing considering the detail, however since filming over a year ago now the museum has undergone even more work and is set to be a really amazing place for the public to visit. Each room has been filled with curiosities, both weird and wonderful from all over the world, some with celebrity connections. Zak's collection does indeed rival ours I have to say. The first area we entered was the hallway complete with fireplace, which is adorned with skulls and a large portrait of Zak himself. Very Addams family I thought! Everyone took their positions and Casey explained that I needed to walk directly down the hallway holding Peggy before turning into a small waiting area, which looked just like ordinary bookcases. So, I had my orders and waited for action! It's amazing when you witness a TV production being made.

The time and effort that goes into every tiny detail is mind boggling and quite frankly I highly doubt I'd have the patience to work in that world. After a few takes we got "the walk" right and I waiting in a small square area with bookcases along 3 of the walls. I didn't know what I was waiting for, then suddenly the largest bookcase began to move! It was opening to reveal a secret room with candelabras, blue and purple lighting and 2 large wooden high backed thrones in which Zak and I were to sit. There was an old wooden childs seat placed next to me which I was asked to place Peggy in to. At this point she still had their black bag over her head and I admit I felt kind of foolish. I glanced at Aaron (Goodwin) who was controlling a camera directed on me and he winked as if to say "you're doing great" so I felt at ease.

I couldn't help but notice Zaks immediate discomfort at seeing Peggy. Up to this point he hadn't seen her, as the production team has requested that she be kept in her large bag. Zak seemed a little lost for words and for a short time we looked at each other in that awkward way you do when you don't know who is going to speak first. Obviously Zak did. He began by asking me to explain who I was and who I'd bought to his museum. The interview continued for a while but far from settling around Peggy, Zak seemed increasingly unsure of her, and when I mentioned that I'd worked with haunted objects for 17 years and had never experienced anything like Peggy, he seemed even more uneasy. He was toying with the idea of removing the bag throughout our interview but there was part of me that didn't really know if he would do it. In between takes we sat and talked about various things, while Aaron went outside for his cigarette breaks. I had no preconceptions about either Aaron or Zak prior to meeting them. I'd never been a huge Ghost Adventures fan, although I had watched a few episodes, and so I didn't know what to expect from either of them. After spending a small amount of time in their company I can tell you that they are very different in many ways, but they share their sense of humour, which is why they're such good friends I guess. If I had to describe them briefly I'd say one of them is reserved and intense, the other is confident and very cool. I'll leave you dear reader to decide which is which. One of the strange things to happen while Zak and I were speaking on film was that we seemed to be being bombarded by flies as soon as Zak began suggesting that Peggy may not like attention. It was very sudden and they were really invasive, constantly landing on our faces while we were trying to speak, Zak more so. He commented that it was odd and Aaron said that in all his time in Vegas he didn't think he'd ever seen a fly! Where they were coming from or why we just couldn't work out but it was at best distracting and at worst quite worrying. Zak made reference to the fact that it is common in cases of demonic presence to get these infestations, which didn't make me feel very comfortable as you can imagine! We took a break as the flies were getting too intense and affecting the filming.

When we resumed Zak began suggesting that we remove the bag from Peggy. At that moment there came a shout out from Billy Tolley in the control room to say that the camera directed at Peggy had suddenly switched itself off, while all others were working perfectly. Zak rushed into the room to see for himself and sure enough Peggys camera had gone off. Zak speculated this may be Peggy not wanting to be shown, but finally he requested that we remove the bag, but not before asking me to make sure her head was facing away from him.

In his words he didn't want a heart attack. I was asked by the producer to stand behind Peggy and very slowly lift the bag. In my minds eye I could imagine how this moment would be edited to incorporate dramatic music and camera angles to be quite a suspenseful few seconds, but truthfully it was just as intense in reality as it was on camera. Once Peggy had been revealed I sat back in my chair and waited. I looked at Aaron, I looked at Zak and glances were exchanged between us all for a few moments. It felt like forever. It was one of those times in life when you feel like something is about to happen. You're almost waiting for a loud noise or for something to scare you. I could see Zak quietly taking a few deep breaths and Aaron was shaking his head and whispered "there's no way I'm looking at her dude".

We wrapped up my interview and I was asked to leave Peggy in her position while I made my way back off set. At this point Katrin was asked to go through to chat with Zak. To this day I have no idea how that really went as Katrin didn't talk about it. When she returned she seemed relieved that it was over but also a little bit distressed. I think she was shocked to see Peggy sitting on set, as no-one had warned her. I confess I hadn't even considered the possibility that she would be so fearful, and I certainly didn't think that she'd have such strong reactions to being close to the doll. It was immediately after Katrins interview that something very strange happened.

Simon, Katrin and I were sitting around a table off set when Jami came through and asked if we could all wait outside as something was going on. We exchanged a puzzled look before standing and making our way outside, leaving Peggy. Jami walked us to a bench in the garden area but couldn't tell us anything. We sat for a while discussing how odd it all seemed and as the sun began to go down, and the December chill started to creep around us I started wondering what the hell was happening.

At some point, maybe 30 or 40 minutes after leaving the set fresh coffee was provided again but no one could really tell us what was going on. Most of the production team genuinely didn't seem to know and so we didn't want to press them, so changed the subject. I would estimate that we were outside for approximately an hour before Jami came out and told us we could go back inside.

When we were called through back onto set we were shown to a different room, a room set up for a séance. It was full of candles and various divination tools and looked great. Patti Negri was now in charge in this room and sat at the head of the table.

Already seated at the table were Zak and Jay Wasley who I was yet to speak to.

Zak asked me to place Peggy in the chair between Jay and Patti, which I did. As I was doing so he asked that I make sure she was facing away from him again, but by now I knew this was what he was comfortable with and so I'd already placed her at a slight angle. I sat down next to Zak and he apologized for the weird delay earlier and told me that he'd experienced some strange feelings and emotions as a result of being close to Peggy, involving anger and rage but he didn't want to talk too much about it so I didn't ask for details. I realized that this was the reason we had been quickly ushered out of the building earlier, and since Deadly Possessions aired, we have learned the full extent of his experience.

Zak explained his reasons for wanting to conduct a séance and we all settled in. At this point Katrin wasn't present, but when we were ready Zak went to find her. As he led her into the séance room she looked like a rabbit in the headlights. Sheer terror across her face and when she saw Peggy she froze to the spot. We were all waiting at the table but it took a while for Katrin to come close enough to sit down. Zak reassured her that she could leave the séance at any time if she felt too uncomfortable, and so we all held hands and began.

I won't detail every moment of the séance as it's best watched for yourself on the show, but during that séance a few things happened which made me personally convinced that we were not only in the presence of someone or something from the spirit realm, but also that Patti was indeed receiving information from the other side. We had candles which appeared to dance when asked, in particular a row of 3 candles behind Jay were, at one point flickering in turn as if someone was running their hand across the top them one at a time. Zak also commented that the tea light candles on the shelves seemed to be burning down much quicker than usual and we all noticed the wax was dripping quickly down the shelves behind Patti in a way it just wasn't doing anywhere else in the room. Patti and Jay also heard the old vintage typewriter behind Peggy clicking as if someone was trying to type something.

For me the strangest thing I personally experienced was the rocking of my chair, which it turned out Katrin was also experiencing. I looked at Zak and said it felt like a dog was passing underneath the chair and when he looked he said he could see the movement too. Patti described a very strong energy, a female energy and also a male. As she was talking about the male spirit she described him as dark, and her voice started going croaky. She explained that she felt like her airways were being constricted as if someone didn't want her to speak. She said this is how a lot of people will feel if they connect to the spirits around the doll, and said it's likely that they will feel pain in the throat and chest.

As the séance wound down Patti blessed us all and closed the session.

Zak explained that he wanted Katrin to remain in the room with Patti to hopefully gain some closure in respect of her feelings about Peggy. Zak, Jay and I left the room and waited just outside. While the cameras were rearranging their angles I started chatting to Jay and he asked me about living in England. He told me his family were originally from the Isle of Man, somewhere I've never been but always wanted to go to.

He himself had never been and we chatted away about how quaint it must be quite oblivious to what was going on in the room next door. Zak came over to us and before he could speak I told him that I'd had no idea she was so afraid of Peggy. I felt a sense of guilt about putting her in a situation in which she clearly felt so uncomfortable.

"You've never met her before have you?" he checked. "No never" I confirmed.

After passing a few more comments about how terrifying the doll is to her we decided to make our way back to the doorway to oversee what was going on. What I saw was something I was not expecting. Katrin was hugging Peggy.

It felt like a good end to the show and Katrin left happy and much calmer.

I checked my watch and it was 8.30pm. After a 12 hour day I assumed that would be it and we would say our goodbyes and be taken home. It was explained to me that they'd had to wait for nightfall to film the 'arrival scenes' in which I would approach the house carrying Peggy, knock on the door and be shown in by the Butler Theodore (a lovely guy called Keith who was full of stories about Las Vegas and his time as a musician in between takes. Since Deadly Possessions aired on April 2nd 2016 we have learnt that shortly after filming our episode on December 7th, Keith suffered a stroke on New Years Eve. Some say it was his mocking of Robert the Doll on episode 1 when they filmed in October, and maybe it was.

Although Peggy was the last object he encountered prior to the stroke, and considering what happened before to people following a meeting with her, I can't help but wonder. I've never publically voiced my feelings about that and I wish Keith the speediest of recoveries. He has had several rehab sessions to work on his speech and is at this moment in time, doing well).

At this point I was shattered and just wanted to go to bed. Still jet lagged and surviving on 2 hours sleep in the last 2 days was beginning to take its toll. But we had to get it done. I went outside with Peggy and waited while large statues were placed either side of the door and blue lighting was set up to give a suitably eerie effect. I was given detailed direction about how to walk, how to hold Peggy, how to knock the door, how to look through the spy hole and once in the house, how to look around. The crew had a very definite idea for the feel of this show, that much was obvious and I was impressed at the effort that had gone into in its prior planning. After 4 or 5 attempts at correctly knocking the door (you wouldn't imagine it could be so difficult!) we had nailed it and just a few photographs later we were being driven back to the hotel, along with Patti who it turned out was also staying at Palms Place. In the car we chatted about the experiences we'd had throughout the day, but I was subdued. In some ways I felt Peggy had been done a disservice through our participation.

Once back in our room with Peggy the surreal aspect of the whole day suddenly washed over me and I felt like I had been in a daydream. I'm sure that extreme fatigue played a part that night as Simon and I slept soundly, which was unexpected, but very welcome. The following day we spent taking in more of Vegas before boarding our evening flight home. We were offered the chance to go back to the set to get some photos with Zak but Simon and I declined, choosing instead to take in more of Las Vegas. Peggy was carefully repackaged and left with the hotel concierge to be collected by couriers the next day. It had been an exhausting, fascinating and unforgettable 5 days, and now all we could think about was getting home to our girls.

Chapter 10
~ Olivias Stroke ~

Over Christmas and New Year, following our trip to Las Vegas, things were quiet. Once Peggy arrived back home things were notably peaceful and at one point I wondered if our time spent with Zak and his team, and especially Pattis séance, had somehow crossed Peggy and the male spirit over into the light...or maybe even held them there in Zaks museum!

However, on February 27th it seemed either one, or both of the

spirits we had grown accustomed to were very much still present around the doll, or at the very least whatever energy the doll seemed to emit was as potent as ever.

Olivia Taylor, a trainee paranormal investigator with Rembrandt Investigation Services based in Bliss Gate, UK contacted me in late January asking if anyone had ever conducted a lone vigil with Peggy, other than myself. We exchanged a few emails and she explained to me that she was currently developing her skills and experience in the field of paranormal investigation and was keen to learn more in particular about haunted objects. She reminded me of myself in the early days and so I decided that if I were to even consider the prospect of leaving her alone with Peggy, then we needed to meet face to face to talk further.

We arranged to meet in the quiet market town of Bewdley near Kidderminster the following week, as it was more or less an equal distance from where we both lived. As I approached the coffee shop we'd agreed on I saw someone sitting in the window already nursing a steaming mug of hot chocolate and anxiously watching people walk past. I knew it was Olivia, and that she was feeling nervous. After ordering my Chamomile tea (one of my new years resolutions was to drink less coffee!) I made my way over to her table.

"Are you Olivia?" I asked with a smile.

"Yes!" she said with a relieved sigh. Often when meeting someone new for the first time, whether you are actually nervous or not, there is a degree of anticipation for their arrival followed by an immediate sense of relief when they appear. I didn't want to draw things out any longer than necessary as I got the feeling she desperately wanted to ask me about Peggy but maybe felt we should exchange pleasantries first.

"So how did you hear of Peggy?" I asked to get the ball rolling. Olivia went on to tell me that she had seen an article in the Shropshire Star newspaper about Peggy and the effects that her video had been having on people, and admitted that initially she had been looking for ways to debunk it. She had searched online and been on various forums reading through conversations from people all over the world. Some who believed in this type of phenomenon, and of course some who didn't. She had really done her homework and knew a lot about our involvement with psychic mediums, the spiritualist church and the fact that we were trying to search through historical records to find out more about possibly identifying our Peggy. Her time spent researching the case had spiked her curiosity further and after much deliberation and discussions with her family she had decided that she would approach me about her idea. I admired her honesty and motivation and began to see that far from being an impulsive decision, this had been something that had been brewing with her for a while and was something that she had unquestionably been debating with herself. She explained that she knew the potential risks and was ready for any consequences, in the name of paranormal exploration and experience.

I wanted to make sure she was fully informed, as there are countless incorrect articles out there, especially online, in relation to Peggy. We discussed the experiences of Katrin Reedik, of the dogs, Patricia Redmonn, Zak Bagans and Patti Negri and of the hundreds of others who had been in touch with me. We sat for 3 hours mulling over things, and giving our thoughts and opinions on some of the experiences. By 5pm I was leaning much more towards letting this go ahead than I had been that morning, however I would still need more time, and I knew that I would need to speak with Simon about it too. We parted company and I promised that I would let her know the following day. Logistically I knew that if we did proceed with the 'experiment', for want of a better word, it might not be the best idea for Olivia to have Peggy in her home. She had told me she had 2 small dogs and while it was fine for Olivia to knowingly place herself in a potentially vulnerable or unpredictable situation, I explained to her that given the severe experiences of other peoples dogs she may be better off not exposing her dogs to the potential dangers. It sounds crazy to say aloud that there may be "potential dangers' with something as seemingly harmless as a plastic doll. But Peggy is not your average plastic doll, and she has demonstrated in more ways than one, that she is by no means harmless.

That evening Simon and I discussed my meeting with Olivia, and he agreed that she seemed well informed and mentally prepared for the vigil. His concern was around her health and we decided that in order for us to go ahead we would need some basic health checks performed, purely for our own peace of mind. After all, it would be completely negligent of us to expect someone with a weak heart for example, to spend a night alone with a haunted object that had already possibly caused 1 heart attack. We would be doing not only Olivia but also ourselves as professionals a great disservice. I telephoned Olivia the following morning and ran the idea of having a basic health check past her. She was over the moon that we were edging closer to letting her do this and was more than wiling to do whatever we needed to feel confident. Again, looking back it seems extreme and over the top to have someone health checked out prior to letting them participate in a paranormal experience, but it's infinitely better to be safe than sorry. Olivia booked in with her GP 3 days later for what she called an "MOT" and so we waited. Hazel had been fairly quiet over the course of the previous week but I suddenly received a telephone out of the blue from her asking what was going on with Peggy lately. I explained that we were actually arranging an overnight vigil for a volunteer when she interrupted me.

"So that's what it is!" she cried. "What?" I asked.

"I had a dream last night Jayne, someone whispered in my ear saying 'wait and see what I can do'. I didn't know what it meant but I woke up thinking of Peggy".

"Wait and see what I can do?" I repeated.

"Yes. It was in a mocking tone, almost like they were boasting. I don't know, might be nothing…just be careful" she said.

I admit I was a little rattled, but after speaking with Olivia in detail on the phone the following day, she remained adamant that she was ready to do this, and so it was all arranged.

Rather than have Peggy in her home, we decided it was best to find a neutral location and arranged a room for Olivia at a small hotel close to her town. The logic behind this was that if Olivia did decide it was all too much for her, or had a sudden change of heart for any reason, she could simply pack her bag and go home. We would collect Peggy the following day. Part of me was also keen not to encourage whatever spirit or spirits were present to form a bond or connection to Olivia and being in her home, her personal private space, may have left the vigil with loose ends. I took Peggy to the hotel about an hour before Olivia arrived and got her settled. By this I mean we placed her on a chair in the corner of the room and set up a few pieces of equipment around her. Motion detectors, an EMF meter, 2 audio recorders and a few trigger objects to be precise. When Olivia arrived she too had bought along equipment and after 30 minutes or so the room was well and truly ready for the evening ahead. We sat and went over a few 'house rules' regarding Peggy, which included a request that she not be touched. We don't normally do this, but as Olivia would be completely isolated and alone with the doll I personally felt it was an added precaution and, one which Olivia was happen to agree to.

After leaving a bottle of holy water on the dressing table, and giving one final glance back at Peggy we left the room and made our way along the corridor.

Looking back my recollection is vivid. I had the feeling of being watched the entire time we were in that hotel, and not from guests or the staff. It was like someone was literally standing right behind me. I could almost feel them sending shivers through my spine. Maybe it was all in my mind given the circumstances, but if time working on this case has taught me anything, it is to never ignore those subtle sensations that only seem to come when you're possibly in the presence of something unseen.

What happened in the 6 hours from when we left the hotel at roughly 8.30pm until we received a distressed telephone call at 2.33am, is best explained by Olivia herself and so what follows is her statement.

I couldn't believe my luck when Jayne called me to say they'd decided to let me spend alone time with Peggy. I know it can't have been an easy decision but from meeting Jayne in person I knew that she was as intrigued in the idea as I was, although she was very hesitant. Once I knew I'd be doing the lone vigil I suddenly felt nervous. I wondered if I was doing the right thing, but then I think you always feel like that when you're about to embark upon something new and scary.

When I met Jayne and Si at the hotel they had got Peggy ready, and all I had to do was set up my equipment. I'd decided not to take many things, being on my own I thought it would be interesting to try to use my own senses as much as possible rather than relying on my gadgets. Jayne had explained that I shouldn't pick Peggy up, or touch her unless I'd asked aloud and felt I'd received a definite sign that it was ok. I decided to air on the side of caution and not even ask to be honest.

I'd say the first 2 or 3 hours were quite uneventful. I did get some fluctuations in temperature at odd, inconsistent times and had checked the air conditioning, which was off, so there wasn't really an explanation. I kept making notes, every time something happened, thinking that maybe when I looked back over them to next day there might be a correlation or something. It was around 12.15am when I first noticed the shaking.

I'd be questioning Peggy aloud about who she was, whether she could confirm how many fingers I was holding up by giving the correct number of taps, that kind of thing. I tried to write down the fact that I'd suddenly gone incredibly cold down my right side, and that the EMF meter had registered a change in the energy of the room when tingling started in my wrist, then spread up my arm. I assumed it was just the shivers as the room had gone much colder, but it didn't stop. I ran my hand under warm water in the bathroom but still it wouldn't stop. In the end I sat on my hand and after about 3 minutes or so I felt it had calmed down, but I was feeling uneasy and watched. I tried to pick up my pen but my right arm was very weak and felt like I'd been laying down on it all night, like pins and needles, or what some people call a 'dead arm'. I've never had anything like that happen before. I went to my bag to get my bottle of water but my arm and right side felt so weak by this point that I couldn't open the zip. I was beginning to panic. I went right over to Peggy, stared her directly in the eyes and asked "are you doing this?". I don't remember much of what happened after that except that I had a sudden sharp pain in my head and the arm that had been tingling went completely numb. I lay on the end of the bed and suddenly the room was spinning. I had no sense of time at all. It could have been a minute it could have been an hour. At some point I felt I had enough strength to reach for my phone, which was on the floor and to this day I have no idea how it got there. Maybe I'd had it in my other hand and dropped it, I can't remember. I called Jaynes number but I don't remember saying anything. I think I blacked out, or maybe fell asleep on the end of the bed, as the next thing I remember is seeing people dressed in green (I soon realized they were paramedics) being let into the room by the hotel staff, followed by Jayne and Si. I could hear the paramedics asking me if I could speak but it didn't make any sense to me. I know I was taken to hospital, which is where I woke up the following day around 1pm they tell me. The experience has luckily left me without any permanent side effects or damage. Apparently I'd suffered a sudden lack of oxygen to the brain, which could have been fatal. There is no proof that it was linked to something paranormal. But the odds are stacked strongly towards the suggestion that it was. What are the chances of someone young like me having a stroke on the same night they try making contact with a powerful spirit, and literally at the moment I asked Peggy if she was doing it?

The experience hasn't put me off paranormal work, if anything I'm more curious now than ever but as for Peggy, I won't be getting involved again. No offense to Jayne or Si but I don't see the point in risking my life and if anyone else is thinking of doing what I did…JUST DON'T".

Olivia Taylor Rembrandt Paranormal

Chapter 11
~ "Deadly Possessions" airs ~

a few tweets made during the show

On April 16th 2016 episode 3 of Deadly Possessions aired in the US featuring Peggy in the first half. I must admit I was nervous to see how the show had been edited and whether or not most of what I'd said had been cut out. I knew Peggy would have a 20-minute window in the show, and considering we had been filming for over 12 hours, also knew that a lot of what happened would end up, as they say, on the cutting room floor due to time restrictions.

In the week leading up to the showing of the episode, I was made aware of an interview with Zak for Dread Central, in which Zak claims that he got a "really bad vibe" from me during our interview. I found this really odd and throughout the entire day there had been no obvious tension, other than Zak feeling noticeably uncomfortable around Peggy. This disturbed me, as I was now concerned that for some reason the show was going to portray me as the reason for Peggys activity, like some kind of occult practitioner or something! Zak had suggested in his comments that some owners of haunted objects are involved in witchcraft or darker arts and often use their objects during rituals. I couldn't quite believe what I was reading, but told myself that there has to be a degree of tension building in the lead up to any show and so put it to the back of my mind. It goes without saying that I've never been involved with anything connected to the more sinister side of the Occult, and would certainly never try to involve Peggy, or any other object in anything so dangerous.

With the time difference it was Sunday morning when I saw the response to the episode online. From the live Twitter conversation going on throughout the show is was clear that an overwhelming number of people had been terrified to look at Peggy when her face was revealed. I scrolled down as many comments as I could but the sheer volume of them was incredible, causing #Deadly Possessions to trend for the first time. Below are a few comments taken from those initial reactions, for which I have sought permission to share.

After watching Peggy the doll I got severe pains and had to go the hospital

Linkhylianknight via Twitter

I felt a pressure in my head/dizzy and a warm blood rush from my head to my toes after looking at Peggy the doll

Nicky Kyker via Twitter

OK, well watching #PeggyTheDoll last night, my mother suffered an aneurysm. She's in hospital right now. Was during the séance.

Jenny Donaldson via Twitter

My head is just pounding! I felt you Zak, with the anger. For real. She is pretty powerful.

Melissa Manzella via Twitter

It seemed that "Peggy-mania" had taken over Twitter. I was flooded with emails, messages and friend requests and quite honestly I began to wonder what I'd unleashed! People were sending me photographs of scratches, burn marks, and medical reports informing me that they had suffered as a result of staring directly at Peggy. I began to wonder if many of these were genuine, although medical reports from Paramedics and Hospitals can't be argued with. I'd asked a friend of mine Ffion to do some research for us as part of another project and she had kindly also agreed to help monitor and manage Peggys facebook group as requests to join were hitting the hundreds daily, and I wanted to make sure the group didn't descend into a circus. After a while it was suggested that I should create a separate page for Peggy on Facebook so that people could post their experiences themselves rather than sending me emails, and I thought it was a great idea and would certainly free up some of my time. It was created and almost immediately people began sharing what had happened to them, they believed as a result of seeing Peggy. Then a bombshell struck. A photograph appeared of Katrin Reedik lying in a hospital bed. My stomach churned as I began to read what had happened. Katrin had watched the episode, and it had led her to think about Peggy again. She began feeling unwell and the result was a suspected stroke. She had little movement in her right arm and not for the time was now in hospital. I couldn't believe it. I'm not sure why, as she wasn't the first person to have a stroke possibly connected to Peggy, but after her heart attack, and the work Patti Negri had done with her, albeit briefly, to assist her in breaking the connection with the spirits that inhabit the doll, I honestly thought she would be fine. It seemed that maybe whatever spirits or energies were around the doll were having a definite affect on Katrin and they weren't about to let her go so easily. I contacted Patti concerned for Katrins health and she assured me that once Katrin was back home she would get in touch and do some really solid in depth spiritual work with her to break this toxic bond once and for all. Patti explained that these things sometimes take more than one attempt, much like an exorcism. I continued to check in with Katrin and Zak sent prayers via Twitter as did many of his followers. A couple of weeks later someone tweeted to Zak asking him which object had affected him the most. His response was unsurprising...

Tweet

Zak Bagans ✓
@Zak_Bagans

As crazy as it sounds. Peggy.

> **Helen Susan Wherry** @Helenswuk84
> @Zak_Bagans What item from #DeadlyPossessions would you say that has affected you the most? xx

30/04/2016 9:03 am

61 RETWEETS **314** FAVORITES

The public reaction to Peggy was more intense than I'd expected although I knew there would be a number of people genuinely affected, and a number simply looking for attention. As a result of the sheer volume of reports we began receiving we decided that in order to pursue any of them further or even take them seriously, we needed evidence. Something from the person getting in touch to show us that this experience they claimed to have had, really did happen. And so we began asking for medical reports from those who said they'd been hospitalized. I didn't expect to get any come back, but sure enough, the scanned copies began arriving in our inbox. At the same time, we started being asked by several paranormal organisations to attend their events and conferences with Peggy. This made us uneasy. We'd seen what had happened to Olivia Taylor, to Katrin, to Zak and to countless others across the world. Simon felt that knowingly exposing more and more people to the potential ill effects of the doll was definitely not a good idea, and I agreed. We decided that if we couldn't fully understand who or what was attached to the doll and subsequently aid in crossing them over into the world of spirit, then our long-term plan would be to contain the energy and hopefully the activity in the hope that it would prevent further people being hurt. In other words, we were considering sealing Peggy in a custom cabinet forever.

Chapter 12
~ Paris...flies again? ~

As is often the way with media arrangements, requests for appearances can often come at short notice. I had received an email from a lady named Candice Jacquet Ferrari, from French TV network Canal+ at the end of April asking if I would be willing to fly to Paris to be interviewed by Antoine Du Caines (best known for his days as the Eurotrash presenter) for his TV show L'emission D' Antoine. I was reluctant. I'd seen Eurotrash and knew that generally speaking it was nothing more than a freak-show where guests were the subject of ridicule and mockery.

I felt pretty certain that I didn't want to be part of that kind of production. I voiced my concerns to Candice who was very reassuring and sent me a number of links to previous shows so that I could judge for myself. She explained that the show has a mixture of both light hearted, and also serious topics and that this particular episode was focused on the Paranormal. She said the interview would be one to one in front of a live audience and that they would want me to take along some dolls from my collections, ideally Peggy. Although I was 50/50 about going, what I did know without a shadow of doubt was that IF I did agree, I wouldn't be taking Peggy or any doll for that matter. It took a week or so of discussions to convince me to say yes, but in the end I did agree. They seemed so eager for my participation and had answered all of my questions and concerns that I felt comfortable enough with the idea. After some negotiations, they booked my hotel and plane ticket and I penciled the show in for May 4th. I'd asked for an idea of Antoines questions prior to arrival in Paris so that I could ensure the interview wouldn't be overly comical. To my surprise, Antoine is actually quite interested in the whole phenomena and was genuinely interested in learning more, alongside making an entertaining show for his viewers of course. Instead of taking along dolls, I had agreed to take along some pieces of technical equipment commonly used in paranormal investigations and the plan was that I would explain how they work. I took an EMF meter and the P-SB7 Spirit box, which as it turned out I didn't need to use. I arrived in Paris at just after 4pm and was met by a driver at the airport who would be taking me to my hotel in the centre of Paris. It was a warm, pleasant day and as we drove passed the Eiffel tower while chatting about the supernatural in broken French I felt very blessed to have so many opportunities as a result of following my passion.

As a 17 year old girl going along on my first investigation with friends, I could never have imagined that in years to come I would have made it my lifes work.

We pulled up at the hotel, and once in my room I felt very alone. Simon was unable to make the trip with me, and for just 1 night it wasn't really practical either and so here I was, alone in Paris with several hours to kill before the car would arrive to drive me to the TV studios. I decided that the best use of the time would be a relaxing bath followed by a good meal. I knew I didn't need to spend time making myself presentable as they had allocated an hour for hair and make-up, although I hoped it wouldn't take quite that long to get me camera ready!

I tried to relax and soak up the effortlessly chic Parisian ambience, but in the back of my mind I was nervous about what was to come. I needn't have been but then I'm a natural born worrier I'm afraid.

At 8pm my car arrived and off we went through the city centre traffic. I hadn't realized that it was actually a holiday weekend in France and so the streets were gridlocked by people desperately trying to escape the hustle and bustle for some peace and quiet. As we approached the studios the driver asked me if I worked in fashion.

With a confused expression I replied "No, why?".

He explained that Canal+ were a large fashion company as well as having a TV network, something which I had no idea about, but then I can't claim to have ever been at the cutting edge of what is or is not considered fashion. As we approached the studios I was surprised at how large they were and how modern and classy the whole set up was. I had been told that I'd be taken to a VIP green room where there would be a free bar and buffet for me to help myself to, but what I had in mind, and what actually materialized were very different, and I have to say I was very pleasantly surprised.

The buffet consisted of gorgeous French cheeses, cold meats, sushi rolls and much more, and the bar was very tempting.

Unfortunately by this point, the idea of a live studio audience had set my nerves on edge and the anxiety I was now feeling meant there was little chance of me enjoying either food or alcohol, and while a stiff drink may have settled my nerves, I stuck to soft drinks and anxiously waited. The production crew rushed around speaking French leaving me without a clue what was going on, and I felt that I stuck out like a sore thumb. After about 30 minutes I was shown to make up, where I was powdered, glossed, primped and preened in preparation before being introduced to my interpreter for the evening. And was I glad to see her! I was given an earpiece to receive her translations through, and a mic and waited backstage. I watched as Antoine and the team set up a mock séance in which Antoine was dressed as Elvis being projected on a big screen through to mists of time, and although it was in French, I still found it all quite amusing.

A few moments before the interview, Antoine ran to get changed into his suit, and came back to introduce himself. He apologized for the jovial elements of the show and explained to me that he would be bringing a doll on to the stage just for entertainment and seemed keen to assure me it was just a bit of fun and in no way trying to mock the subject. I warmed immediately to Antoine. He is down to earth and welcoming and seems to really care about his guests opinion of his show. The stage was wheeled in, chairs were set up and I was directed towards my chair. An image of Peggy came up on the big screen then it was lights, camera, action!

on set at L'Emission D'Antoine 2016

You may be wondering at this point, why I am including all of this in a book dedicated to Peggy. This is why. The interview was going well, and eventually we came onto the subject of Peggy. A huge image of her came up onto the screen and I began speaking about the various experiences that members of the public have had, and how serious some of them had been. As I was speaking, I noticed Antoine wafting his hand around his face.

"It can't be" I thought. When it was his turn to speak I saw the flies on his face and hair! I didn't mention what had previously happened to Zak when I was last interviewed about Peggy but continued answering his questions while he tried to rid himself of the invasive flies. Now of course, as in Vegas, this could have been purely a coincidence. But just like in Vegas, we had experienced no issues with flies throughout the filming up to the point of discussing Peggy, and let's face it, how often do you watch a TV show and see the presenters having to waft flies away from their faces? Not very often.

I had spoken about Peggy on TV just twice and on both occasions this had happened.

As I was driven back to my hotel I couldn't help wondering how or why this might be happening. Was it me? Were the spirits associated with the doll, actually now associated with me too, and following me around? It was an unnerving thought and part of me was convinced, as I settled down to sleep that night in complete darkness, that I would see something or would be aware of a presence in the room. I didn't, and I wasn't. But still the thought remained, and still does.

Chapter 13
~ Molly O'Gradys ~

We had agreed some months prior to the airing of Deadly Possessions to attend an event hosted by SpoohUK, a ghost hunting organization based in Leicester ran by 2 friends Ian Grant Rogers and Nadine English. Originally the event was to be at a place called Abbey House on the site of the old Leicester Abbey. Unfortunately the owners had cancelled their booking at short notice and so as a back up venue, Molly O'Gradys, a Grade II listed building in the heart of Leicester, was chosen. They had asked if we would take Peggy along, and we'd agreed, although cautiously. Had they asked us in the weeks following the airing of Deadly Possessions we'd have undoubtedly decided against it, but the date was set, their guests were expecting her, and Nadine had even gone to the trouble of getting everyone to sign disclaimers in the event of anything happening to anyone.

Their plan was to set up 4 CCTV cameras in a small room focused on Peggy all evening. Guests were to be given a 10 minute lone vigil each with her which would be streamed live via the SpoohUK website. I have to say I didn't expect anything to happen as is usually the way with the spirit world when faced with a lot of people with a lot of expectations, but I hoped Peggy would make herself known at some point.

It was May 14th, the day before our wedding anniversary, and

we got Peggy ready and headed up to Leicester. Having never been to Leicester before we were not prepared for the incredibly difficult one-way systems in place, and navigating ourselves into the centre of the city proved quite a task!

Fortunately we were only about 15 minutes late, and when we walked in, all guests were seated ready and waiting. After a few hellos and hugs we took Peggy to the room they had allocated as hers for the evening and got her into place. As is usually the case when people meet Peggy for the first time, Ian and Nadine were surprised at her size. Nadine was instantly drawn to her and throughout the evening felt very warm towards her, as a small number of people do. I was reminded of a few reactions at Derby Gaol the previous October, when there were similar feelings of wanting to care for her.

Also invited on the event were Lee Steer and Charlene Lowe Kemp from Project Reveal who planned to film the event for their 'Ghosts of Britain' YouTube channel. I had spoken with Lee many times over the previous 2 years and been the subject of one of his web interviews and so it was good to meet in person.

Peggy remained in her room and guests were given their allotted time with her. Some reported feeling touched, feeling slightly sick or had headaches while in the confined space and watching the CCTV cameras we did see a few large orbs, some which seemed to appear as people asked for a sign or in the case of one guest, Karen Rickett, a direct request for an orb! Charlene from Project Reveal also had an odd experience when she found her camera was zooming in on Peggy on it's own at one point which I witnessed for myself too as was standing next to her. She wasn't touching any buttons but suddenly it began zooming in. Something else interesting happened while we were in the room with Charlene, Lee and the Project

Reveal team. With various pieces of equipment set around the room Lee began speaking aloud to Peggy. Lee considers himself skeptical when it comes to the paranormal and so in many ways is the perfect person to attempt this kind of experiment. He was trying to get a reaction and decided to blow on the dolls hair from behind. As soon as he did the static meter, which was on the floor about 2 feet away, suddenly lit up with lights shooting right up to the top indicating a strong sudden change in atmosphere or energy. We had no idea if this meant she liked it, didn't like it, or whether it was just a coincidence but it was something we couldn't explain as the meter hadn't gone off at all before that moment and didn't after.

Towards the end of the evening I gave a talk around Spirit Attachment and our experiences so far with Peggy and was asked several questions by guests all of whom seemed truly intrigued by her. Before we left people wanted their photographs taken with her, which we allowed. We all said our goodbyes and with Peggy safely tucked up in her bag again we left. On the way home we chatted about the experience. In the past we'd found that the introduction of Peggy to a haunted location has led to the resident spirits, for whatever reason, retreating, or going quiet. At Derby Gaol for example, the cells in particular are notoriously active, but when we were there with Peggy, the only energy to come forward and communicate was that of Peggy herself, through the Ouija board. Molly O'Gradys has apparently been one of the most active venues for the Spoohuk team over the years, however during our evening there with Peggy, Ouija boards refused to work, there was no EMF reactions and no-one felt any kind of presence there at all which I imagine was unusual. It has been suggested to us that the level of the spiritual energy associated with the doll, given that there are 2 spirits around her, can alter the usual balance of a place, which I can understand. Another theory is that the darker, male energy is literally terrifying most other spirits simply by it's presence. We don't know, and of course it's only theorizing, but we couldn't deny that this was not the first time that the doll had seemed to act as a blocker for the usual spiritual activity in a known haunted location.

Left to Right: Nadine English, Peggy, Ian Grant Rogers, Simon and myself

Chapter 14
~ A tough decision ~

There has always been a degree of inner turmoil surrounding our guardianship of Peggy (I hesitate to say ownership, as I don't feel we own her). The paranormal is by its very nature unpredictable and at times unfathomable, and so no-one, however experienced, can truly say they know exactly what they are getting involved in 100% of the time. The most seasoned psychic mediums can still be caught off guard from time to time if a spirit is particularly strong or negative. When it comes to the supernatural none of us can ever claim to have 'seen it all'.

In the time we have spent exploring this specific case, the subject of responsibility comes up again and again for Simon and I and we are always incredibly cautious when it comes to allowing people to 'meet' Peggy. We have felt for some time now that we seem to be embroiled in a snowball effect, in that the more people who share the same space as Peggy i.e. the more people that are allowed to interact with whatever is around the doll, the greater the proceeding activity and the more heightened subsequent unexpected phenomena is.

It may well be that in some way maybe the spirits associated with the doll have fed from the energy of the living (something which is accepted as happening in the case of hauntings generally) and so the more heightened emotion, whether fear or excitement, that builds around her, the more likely we all are of experiencing something supernatural. This is all well and good up to a point but at what stage in the process do we say enough is enough and resign ourselves to the notion that we will never fully understand the experiences attributed to this specific haunting, and for the safety of everyone concerned, attempt to minimize rather than maximize any future phenomena, at least when it comes to us personally as caretakers. Our resources are obviously limited and I have often wondered if in some way we have done her a disservice in not being able to give her the spot light and recognition that her unusual and striking case deserves, although we've always done what we have felt in the best interests of her and our paranormal research in general.

Following our outing with Peggy to Leicester, we took the doll along to visit a gentleman named Phillip Lawley in Wolverhampton. Phillip is a private Spiritualist and through word of mouth we had reason to believe he had quite a considerable gift, which he often described as 'his torment'. Phillip does not accept payment for readings and does not advertise. You will not find him online or on social media and it's this amongst other things that appealed to us about having his opinion. Phillip was made aware of our desire to meet him through a mutual friend, and after some persuasion (and a donation from us to the Cats Protection League charity on his behalf) he agreed to see us.

On June 1st at 7pm we took Peggy to a small terraced home in a quiet leafy street in central Wolverhampton. Phillip had gathered a small group of his spiritualist friends, all of whom were apparently undergoing spiritual training to enhance their psychic abilities and so he felt it would be beneficial for them to be part of such an unusual meeting.

Initially I was apprehensive about allowing so many people access to her in that type of setting, so kept

Peggy next too me for the majority of the time we were there. Phillip began by asking everyone, including Peggy, to sit in a circle and link hands. As I reached over and held the small plastic hand next to me I didn't feel how I expected to feel. To some of you reading this it may seem odd to say, but in all the time we've had Peggy, I don't think I've ever held her hand. I don't think I've ever held the hand of any doll in the way I would hold a child's and so it just hasn't ever occurred to me to try this.

Rather than feeling foolish, I felt a sudden sharp shock, similar to the type you get when you touch someone sometimes and describe it as an 'electric shock'. It's clearly not electricity but it takes you by surprise and makes you jump that's the only way I can describe it. It was so unexpected that it did make me jump, which in turn made most of the group jump too.

Naturally immediately following the jump I started to laugh, as now I *was* feeling foolish. Everyone found it quite amusing, some probably even wondered if I was attempting to gain attention, or build up an atmosphere, but I knew what I had felt. I cautiously reached out once more and touched Peggy's hand. This time there was nothing, and so we began.

Phillip recited something in Latin, which I later learnt was the Lords prayer. We sat in silence for what seemed like an eternity until suddenly I began to notice a small light hovering in the centre of the circle. My instant reaction was to scan the room for possible light sources or hiding places for someone with a laser pen. The mind of a paranormal investigator is often littered with suspicion and sadly it tends to be for good reason. As my eyes passed from picture, to shelf, from window to door I could not see what could be causing this light. My secondary thought was to examine the faces of the others present in the room, for signs of recognition. To my surprise no one else appeared to have noticed this light, although throughout my entire appraisal of the room and my fellow sitters, it had remained a constant in the corner of my eye. I recalled previous occasions in which I had bore witness to unexplainable lights – an experience unrelated to this case, immediately came to mind. The first home Simon and I bought together was a 300-year-old cottage in which we experienced a range of unexplainable things, one of which I talked about in an earlier chapter. The experience relating to lights happened in 2009 while I was in the shower. I began to notice small sparkling lights out of the corner of my eye. They were there for no more than 5 seconds, after which I heard the 'click' of the light cord, which was immediately followed by the light going off. I called to Simon to say it was not amusing, but no reply came. Annoyed I got out of the shower, grabbed a towel and looked out of the bathroom door, onto the landing. Simon was nowhere to be seen. I called several times but again, as before, no response. As I walked back into the bathroom I peered through the open window to see Simon at the end of the garden busy cleaning out our chicken coop. I quickly dressed and made my way outside and towards Simon. I told him what had happened and asked if he'd been upstairs. He looked very confused and assured me he hadn't set foot inside the house for a good 30 minutes or more. I knew something very strange had happened. Not only had I seen the light go off, which could ordinarily be put down to a fuse or a bulb issue, but I had heard the light cord click as if pulled by an unseen hand. That was the part I couldn't explain. Upon checking the light in the bathroom, one click and it worked perfectly. So did the lights that preceded the incident with the bathroom light, mean anything? Were they a coincidence, or did they signal spirit presence?

My attention was suddenly drawn back into my current situation when a lady sitting opposite me, a small elderly woman named Mrs Morris, commented that she had suddenly started to feel very cold down her right side. Phillip closed his eyes and I wondered for a moment whether he might be going into a trance in order to perform channeling of some kind.

Rather than speak aloud to any spirit that may be present, in the way I'm used to witnessing, he instead stood up very suddenly, while still holding the hands of the people either side, which as you would expect took them quite by surprise. "Would the person carrying the pouch of salt please remove it from their pocket?" he eventually requested. The group exchanged glances, but no one spoke or moved.

"Would the person carrying the pouch of salt please do as I ask and remove it from their pocket?" he repeated, now in a more hurried tone. I was about to whisper to Simon to ask if it was him, when a young man sitting 2 chairs to my left reached into the inside pocket of his jacket and pulled out a small pouch which appeared to be made of a velvet fabric and placed it on the cabinet behind him. His face flushed and he had the appearance of a naughty schoolboy. There were some muffled comments, most of which seemed to be concerning Phillips ability to know about the salt. I didn't find it particularly amazing however as in these situations it always stands a good chance that someone will have some salt about them somewhere. During public events we've had people with pockets of salt by way of protection, and so I can't say with any degree of certainty that there was anything particularly supernatural about Phillips statement. What followed however, I most certainly do believe was otherworldly or as close to otherworldly as we've ever been.

What I can only describe as a ball of light appeared directly above us all. It was about the size of a tangerine and lasted only a few seconds before fading. Simon later described it as dissolving, which could also be accepted as a reasonable description of what we saw. This light, or what appeared to be a light seemed very pale in colour and very bright. Everyone was fixated on this light, all except Phillip who had his eyes closed and hands raised. To this day I'm not entirely sure of the correct terminology for what we experienced.

As the daylight began to fade outside a couple of hours later Simon and I decided it was time to head home. Nothing more had happened that evening following the light, but everyone commented on how they had felt a close presence once the light had appeared, almost as if it had signaled an arrival.

In the weeks and months that followed I tried researching this strange phenomena and my efforts bore fruit to some degree. I learned that there were theories around energy, and collective consciousness, and that some groups of people claimed to be able to build up such collective energy that it created a visible centre or vortex, when focused with practice. Had I not had the experience at Phillips home with the ball of light, I would have thought this all quite unbelievable, but now I'm not so sure. I know I saw something in that room that day, which appeared physical, by that I mean physically present rather than simply in my own imagination. I only wish now that

I had reached out and tried to touch it, but of course as in most situations, hindsight is a wonderful thing.

We realize that what we have welcomed into our lives, is not only an opportunity to potentially explore and understand elements of the unknown, but also something of intense unpredictability, and while exciting and fascinating, that previously mentioned parental instinct in both Simon and I has started to pull us a more considered direction, and our focus has ultimately became one of safeguarding our family. Some of you reading this may feel it uneccesarily dramatic however cast your mind back a few chapters to the experiences of Olivia Taylor, or to the ongoing health issues of Katrin Reedik and you will hopefully begin to appreciate that for me personally, I now believe that prevention is better than cure and as I have no intention of closing the proverbial stable door after the horse has bolted, I will do whatever I can to ensure my children are safe.

When I received a telephone call from Zak Bagans in January 2017 therefore, I already knew what he was about to ask...and I knew that it was for the best.

Chapter 15
~ Peggy's new 'Father' ~

As I've already discussed, and hopefully by now dear reader you will appreciate, Peggy consumed a large portion of my life and the lives of my family for over 2 years. In that time I have made sacrifices in terms of my children, my home life and my wellbeing. I've travelled, I've talked, I've laughed and I've cried and in many ways I have devoted myself to her story. The affect that such intensive care and study can take on a person cannot be underestimated and towards the end of 2016 I began to feel that I was approaching a crossroads in terms of our journey together. I confess that today my health is not what it was in the years leading up to Peggys arrival and I can't help but consider the possibility that it is my work with her, and possibly even the entities attached to her that have contributed to it's decline.

Quite out of the blue in January 2017 I received an email from Zak asking how we were, and how Peggy was doing. Initially I was unsure that it was genuine as the email address differed to the one I'd been used to. I replied asking if he could call me to chat, and he replied immediately asking if he could call straight away. The time was 8am in the UK and I worked out that it was therefore Midnight in Las Vegas. I knew then that he had something important he wanted to talk to me about, but unfortunately it would have to wait, as most parents will appreciate the school run dominates an otherwise busy schedule! All things revolve around that. I explained that I wouldn't be able to but we arranged to talk later that evening. I spent most of that day considering my response to the question that was inevitably coming. How did I feel about letting Zak look after Peggy? Before I spoke to him at length about it, I'd have said my feelings were mixed. I knew he had a passion for the paranormal (obviously!) and that his new museum was a place he was pouring a lot of his time and energy into. But at the same time I was aware that many of Peggys followers and fans on social media had felt that the way she was treated on Deadly Possessions had been disrespectful and they had been angered in particular at the bag over her head despite my public explanation. I decided to hear his ideas and go with my gut feeling. At around 6pm that evening I was cooking tea and my mobile phone started ringing. It was Zak. I went out into the garden to talk and what he had to say pretty much assured me that this was the beginning of Peggys next chapter.

Zak wanted to give Peggy her very own room in the museum. He explained that the experiences we'd all had during her séance had affected him in such a strong way that he had kept a room for her in the hope that I might allow him to welcome her.. This was clearly something he'd spent a lot of time thinking about over the past 12 months since our visit and I could tell that he had a lot of respect for her. We spoke about a few other things, his upcoming mini series and the fact that he had a month of solid filming and investigating ahead of him, and he told me about a few of the other amazing things he'd acquired for the museum including Michael Jacksons 'Propofol Chair'. He felt that what the museum was lacking, as amazing as it was, was Peggy. I asked for a little time to think about it, and he agreed to email me in a day or 2 and we could discuss it some more, but deep down I knew that I wanted Peggy to get this experience. After all, Zak and his museum have the ability to share her story with infinitely more people than I ever could. And so after some back and forth it was agreed that Peggy would soon be residing in Las Vegas. I explained that there would be some guidelines he would need to follow, and that I would send some of her personal effects along with her. We also discussed future visits and talks as a way of me retaining my contact with her and involvement in her ongoing story. Zak was very excited to share the news with the world that he was "Peggys new Father", and when I awoke the following morning my Facebook and Twitter pages were awash with the story.

Dread Central had the first interview with Zak discussing his acquisition of Peggy and I had a raft of emails and messages from people asking if it were true. The next time I contacted Zak I told him he'd almost broken the internet with the revelation, and I must admit that I was surprised at the speed at which he'd shared the news. He laughed and admitted he'd been so excited he couldn't hold it in. I was only just getting used to the idea myself.

Her departure has been tinged with sadness, after all it's always difficult to let go of any part of your life, knowing that the change will mean that things will never be the same again. However I know that this is not the end of my relationship with Peggy. I am still involved in her care, consulting on peoples experiences and keeping in contact with Zak.

This is merely the beginning of a new chapter in her story, and my instinct tells me that it will be an incredible chapter indeed.

Chapter 16
~ Witness Testimonies ~

Throughout this book that at certain points I have included the relevant testimony, as given to us by the individual concerned. They are in their own words and have not been altered in any way by us. We have collected many during the time we have had Peggy, and in this section I would like to share a few more.

```
Case: Peggy Location: Wigan, UK Date: 20th
April 2015


I was having a dream about a woman who told
me her name was Peggy. As I was staring at
her face trying to make out her features, I
was awoken by my mobile phone ringing,
however when I reached over there were no
missed calls or messages. I instantly
decided to draw the figure I had seen in my
dream. I'm sure it was  her.
```

Linda Winstanley, UK

Case: Peggy

Location: Montreal, Quebec Date: 17th June 2015

Yesterday I was feeling totally drained and light headed and couldn't explain it. It's very unlike me I am usually so full of energy. I now realize a possible cause. I was reading up on Peggy yesterday, and watching your videos of her around noon. Around 1pm was when I began feeling unwell and had to go an lay down which I never do during the day.

I won't be looking at her again, I really felt the effects.

Alana Nickerson

Montreal, Quebec, Canada (originally from NJ)

Case: Peggy

Location: Carrollton, Georgia   Date: 1st December 2015

I accidentally stumbled across something about Peggy last night on my phone. Being someone interested in all things paranormal, of course it peaked my interest. I was reading the article on my phone. I didn't get any pains or negative feelings, only compassion and empathy. I feel bad that whoever Peggy is, she went through what she went through. I researched further and read other articles. During my reading, my phone would frequently suddenly 'not support the page' or 'lose internet connection.' Of course, this could be due to technical issues, but I do find it uncanny that it did this repeatedly during my search and at no other time. What's weird is that I also felt light brushes against my hair and tingly, tickling feelings along my legs, feet, and face. Since I was under the covers, this wasn't due to air conditioning or moving air. It could

still be chocked up to something else but it's rather uncanny I experienced these things while reading about her.

Emery Duffey Georgia

Case: Peggy

Location: Saranac Lake, New York   Date: 2nd December 2015

I had another dream, it started off with me floating in front of a screen, then being sucked literally into a photo of Peggy on the screen. I was frightened, I was being drawn into Peggy. The scene changed and in it I was seeing things from a third person view. There was a lovely woman known by the name Peggy Anne (Miller, later known?) She was walking with a young lad of maybe 13 or 14 wearing grey wool clothes, he had light coloured hair blonde perhaps and he had a cap on his head. The conversation between the two was almost sad, Peggy was bringing her son to a train station, he was going to be leaving her for something mandatory. I watched them walk, something changed Peggy stumbled, she had a vision? Her son noticed, he remarked something about people thinking she was crazy. She sadly looked over at him, he had a lot of animosity towards her for that. Then the scene went black and I heard a loud set of breaks, the very distinct sound of a train stopping, and a medium pitch train whistle.

It was extremely vivid, I could almost see every thread of their clothes, I think there may have been an accident involving the train, she saw something and maybe needs her story to be known.

Tiffany DuQuette New York

Case: Peggy

Location: Warrington, UK Date: April 2016

Friends and followers of Peggy, I've watched videos and looked at photos trying to communicate with Peggy the doll, with my paranormal team, a few times over the last few months, with slight activity on the K2 but nothing more. However, when I saw a recent picture of her about an hour ago I suddenly had a very powerful panic attack and had to hit my bedroom floor very quickly (by the way I haven't had a panic attack for over 3 years now and I've learned to control them very well but as I looked at the photo it really was very sudden and very overwhelming)

Jayne knows I would not fake anything to do with the paranormal, this was a very real experience.

Stephen Bishop Warrington Paranormal

Case: Peggy Location: UK Date: April 2016

I went online to see Peggy and suddenly felt a tightening in my chest and pressure like I couldn't breathe, I then felt a sharp pain and when I looked I had been scratched.

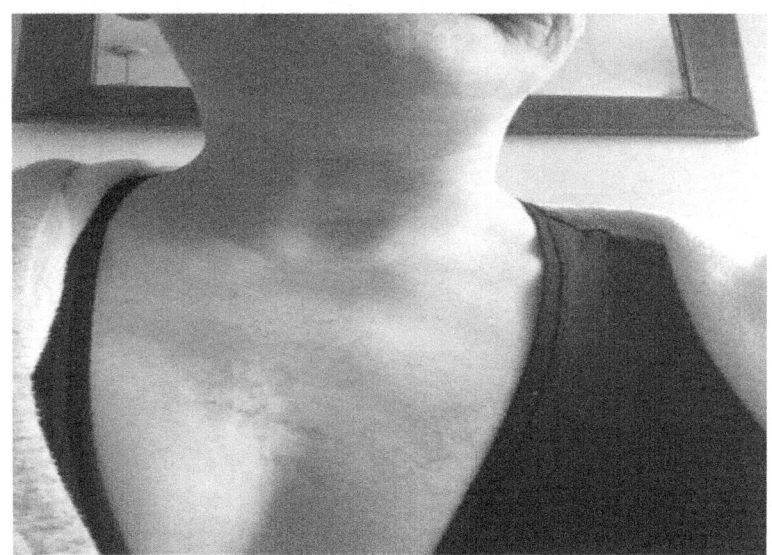

Mila Smith
UK

Case: Peggy

Location: Doncaster, UK Date: April 2016

I thought I'd let you know, my sister watched Zak Bagans with Peggy and a bite mark appeared on her arm. I looked at Peggy and felt fine but my sister got this mark, out of nowhere and we all saw it suddenly appear!

I got my Ouija board out and it spelt out Peggys name when I asked who bit her! My board went crazy it was going around so fast my hands came off the planchette.

My board has never behaved like this before.

- *Statement from Laura McCormick relating to her sister Mary Astari Herne.*

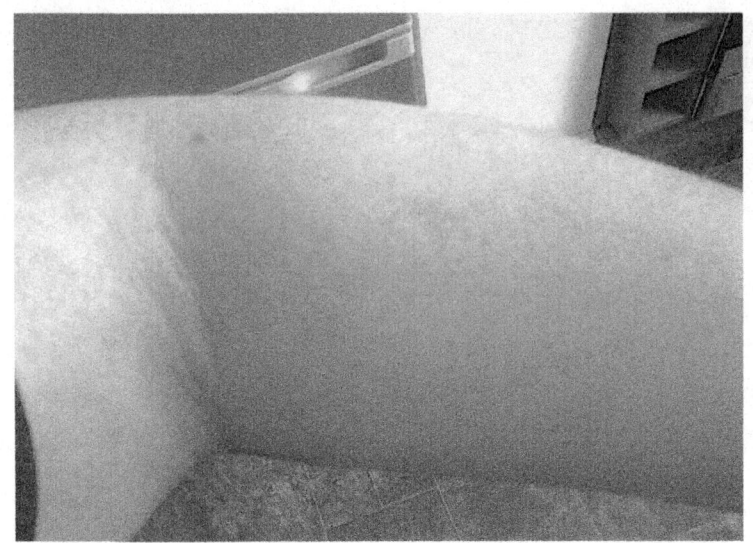

Since getting the bite mark I feel like I have the flu. I have a headache but was fine yesterday before seeing Peggy. Today I can't even lift my head.

– *Update from Mary Astari Herne.*

Laura McCormick & Mary Astari Herne
Doncaster, UK

Of all the hundreds of reports I have now received, one stands out to me as being the most disturbing. Not necessarily because it's dramatic or over the top, but because what this lady has experienced, is eerily similar to my early experience when Peggy first entered our home. This is something I have never spoken about publically and so her experience, for me is all the more valid.

On December 26th 2016 I received the following email:

Hi,

I feel I have to tell you about what I experienced after watching what at first I thought was just another "haunted" doll video with your doll Peggy. I have had paranormal experiences since I was a child, I wouldn't say I'm a medium or psychic but I am sensitive to things around me so I'm not sure if that makes me more likely to be affected. After watching the video almost straight away I was aware that the atmosphere in my home had changed and despite sitting next to a warm radiator I could feel a cold chill and could feel a presence as if someone was standing behind me. I had an uneasy feeling over me for the rest of the evening and when I went to bed that's when the truly disturbing things happened. As I lay in bed I could hear someone moving around my room and when I turned my back I could feel a cold breeze on my face and I was terrified. Every time I started to fall asleep I was having terrible visions of a woman dressed in black with a glowing white face & black eyes. I remember dreaming and in the corner of every dream there she was. I woke during the night screaming (much to the horror of my poor husband). After this, when I woke I was aware that there was a very dark presence in my bedroom standing just inside my bedroom door. I couldn't sleep all night and every time I closed my eyes I was having just terrible visions, this lasted all night. In the morning I got dressed and left my house as I could still feel the dread and was looking over my shoulder and just wanted to get away. I have been out the house all day now but still feel very anxious and am dreading tonight. I have been scared of only one "apparition" during my lifetime but this is different. It is standing in the dark and is terrifying me and I'm not that kind of person!

```
I saw the video on a YouTube top 5 and had
no idea what I was watching or the
reputation of the video and was just hoping
you can give me some reassurance that I'm
not crazy and that this will stop. I am
shocked that the video has the power to do
this and I'm hoping that you can put my
mind at ease,

Thank you Paula Letham UK
```

I didn't see Paula's message until 2 days later, and replied immediately. She informed me that her night terrors had only lasted for 2 days, and stopped once she began avoiding images of Peggy.

Reports of worrying experiences continue to come through to us, the most recent being on January 2nd 2017, which simply read:

```
"Dear Peggy,

I would like to apologise for looking at
pictures of you online without your permission
and I am sorry for not believing that you could
do harm to me. I deeply regret doing what I did
and

I hope that you can somehow forgive me.
Sincerely,

Stephanie Hysquierdo"
```

The message was forwarded directly to me by my website administrator and I responded to Stephanie asking for more information. Her response was as follows.

```
"Hi Mrs Harris,

I've been having very bad chest and shoulder
pains and I even went to the hospital a few
times because of it. I also had a bizarre dream
and I don't remember much of it but I do know
```

that I was in a dark dungeon like room and heard very dark and menacing voices echoing all around me. At first I thought nothing of it but after the pain started to get worse and then I had that dream I thought it was wise to ask for forgiveness from Peggy.

Sincerely"

Now of course this in itself does not constitute evidence that something paranormal was going on for Stephanie, but it's worth noting that once she actively stopped viewing Peggys photos and avoided anything to do with her, the chest pains and nightmares ceased.

In addition to these collated testimonies there are countless reports on YouTube and other social media platforms from people around the world, all of who believe strongly that Peggy has caused them negative experiences. One of the very first came from a lady who wishes to remain anonymous, but whom has given her consent for me to share exactly what happened to her.

Case: Peggy Location: PROTECTED Date: March 2015

Jayne I must tell you that something incredibly frightening has happened to me since I started looking at your photo of Peggy. I didn't want to get in touch at first as I thought you would think I was a crazy person, but please assure me that I'm not alone in this. When I first looked at the photo of the doll I didn't really feel anything other than a nervous feeling in my stomach that I couldn't really explain. I wanted to look away but her eyes were drawing me in.

That night while I was in bed I had my laptop with me and decided to check your page for updates. As I clicked on Peggys photo the screen froze and her image came up huge, like a screensaver, which I couldn't remove.

I began to panic then my candlestick on the other side of the room fell over (luckily the candle had not been lit at the time). I then heard someone breathe directly next to me and it made me jump straight out of bed. I stood in the corner of the room looking back at my bed and I swear I could hear someone slowly walking around my bed. All this time Peggys face was stuck on my laptop screen! The room seemed to go cold and as I live alone I was by this point totally freaking out. I picked up the candlestick and walked towards my bed, not really knowing what I was going to do. I sat on the edge of the bed and started saying the Lords prayer (it's the only prayer I know). As I did the atmosphere seemed to go back to normal but the weirdest thing was that Peggys face went from my screen and my laptop switched off!

Honestly it was the weirdest, most terrifying experience of my life.

Annonymous UK

~ Conclusion ~

When considering a way to conclude this book I must confess that I have struggled. After all how can you offer a conclusion, a summary to something which far from being at and end, could potentially only just be beginning?

When I began working in paranormal investigation in 1998 I didn't really know what I was getting myself into. I was young and full of energy and had an insatiable thirst for knowledge and supernatural experiences. Over the years, while my energy levels may have dipped thanks to a busy lifestyle, children and so on, I have to say that my passion for discovery and for all things unknown has never waivered. Not a moment has passed in those past 19 years where I have considered walking away from this way of life, and let me assure you that a way of life it most certainly is for me. Exploring the paranormal is not a hobby, it is my lifes work and something I dedicate up to 90 hours a week to. It requires patience, dedication and determination…not to mention a very thick skin! You have to be prepared to deal with the criticism of others and the debates that inevitably ensue whenever you tell people the field you work in. But overall I consider myself incredibly blessed, and having Peggy in my life has been a huge part of that blessing.

As I hand over her to care I do so knowing that I have, for the most part, done all I can in terms of studying and understanding her, and I now look forward to taking a watchful backseat, secure in the knowledge that she is never far from my thoughts. After all, it's quite possible that during the time I have had her, I have needed Peggy as much as she has needed me, and in the words of Patti Negri, I will always be her "Mother across the pond". Of course my affection refers only to that lighter energy which many of us have experienced. As for the one I call "the other one", only time will tell what unfolds inside the Haunted Museum.

~ FAQ's ~

No doubt you will have many questions after reading this book. Here I will attempt to offer an insight into my thought processes around this case.

Why don't you just burn the doll?

Firstly, destroying an object will not destroy a haunting. If you believe your house is haunted, burning it down will not destroy the ghosts or the spirits present. A physical act cannot affect the non physical world is such a final way.

Secondly, the attempt to destroy the doll would be incredibly irresponsible and could potentially leave myself, my family or a third party wide open to attachment. In other words, if we destroy the 'vessel' which for whatever reason holds the energy of someone in spirit, how do we know where that energy will transfer to? Human possession is rare, but does happen I believe, and if there was ever a case in which a spirit would be looking for a new 'host', then it would be this one.

Do you ever feel scared of her?

Yes of course! I'd be crazy if I didn't. The world of the unknown is a peculiar and amazing place. We seek answers and truth, but then most of us are only really willing to push the boundaries so far. How many of us would truly want to see into the Afterlife and know for certain what it holds?

Have you got any pets, and if so how do they react?

No I do not. Peggy is the main reason we have decided not to have pets in our home.

Have you ever had nightmares about Peggy?

Yes, but only a few times. In all instances I dreamt of a woman around 50 years old, with blonde hair and piercing dark eyes. She was close to my bed staring directly at me. Each time I awoke in a panic and struggled to sleep again afterwards.

Has Peggy ever moved?

Not that we're aware of other than slightly during the basement video I discussed earlier in the book. This doesn't seem to be a case of a 'chucky-like' doll which can move. The spirits around the doll seem to have no interest in making her perform on demand in that way.

Have you ever had her on display in your home?

No never. She has always been kept away from friends and family, in our basement.

Do you wish you had never had Peggy?

Absolutely not! There have been times when I have wondered if my life would have been better without her, but I know deep down that in deciding to work on her case, I was answering an inner calling and curiosity and that is an opportunity that doesn't come along too often for any of us.

~ About the Author ~

Jayne Harris lives in the peaceful Shropshire countryside with her Husband Simon and 2 daughters.

She is a TV Presenter for UKTV's "Help! My House is Haunted" and has appeared on numerous other shows including "Unexplained: Caught on Camera" and Sky's "Paranormal Captured".

She is a Lecturer, Researcher and keen Historian and in 2016 was named "the UK's foremost female paranormal investigator" by Broadly's 'VICE' magazine.

A prominent figure within the paranormal community and considered a pioneer of studies into Spirit Attachment, Jayne has studied Psychology, Anthropology and Medieval History and is an advocate of lifelong learning having developed 2 paranormal training courses, most recently the accredited 'Applied Paranormal Research' training course available through her website.

Her favourite haunted location is Edinburgh's Old Town.

Jaynes work can be found on her website and social media pages

www.jayne-harris.com

www.hdparanormal.com

Twitter

@hdghost_girl

Facebook

Official Jayne Harris

HD Paranormal

Instagram

HDghost_girl

Made in the USA
Monee, IL
24 October 2021